Contents

Sausage, kale & gnocchi one-pot

Prep:5 mins **Cook:**15 mins

Serves 4

Ingredients

- 1 tbsp olive oil
- 6 pork sausages
- 1 tsp chilli flakes
- 1 tsp fennel seeds (optional)
- 500g fresh gnocchi

- 500ml chicken stock (fresh if you can get it)
- 100g chopped kale
- 40g parmesan, finely grated

Method

STEP 1

Heat the oil in a large high-sided frying pan over a medium heat. Squeeze the sausages straight from their skins into the pan, then use the back of a wooden spoon to break the meat up. Sprinkle in the chilli flakes and fennel seeds, if using, then fry until the sausagemeat is crisp around the edges. Remove from the pan with a slotted spoon.

STEP 2

Tip the gnocchi into the pan, fry for a minute or so, then pour in the chicken stock. Once bubbling, cover the pan with a lid and cook for 3 mins, then stir in the kale. Cook for 2 mins more or until the gnocchi is tender and the kale has wilted. Stir in the parmesan, then season with black pepper and scatter the crisp sausagemeat over the top.

Chicken cacciatore one-pot with orzo

Prep:5 mins **Cook:**55 mins

Serves 4

Ingredients

- 2 tbsp olive oil
- 4-6 skin-on, bone-in chicken thighs
- 1 onion , finely sliced

- 2 garlic cloves , sliced
- 250ml red wine
- 2 bay leaves

- 4 thyme sprigs
- 2 rosemary sprigs
- small bunch of parsley , stalks and leaves separated, finely chopped
- 2 x 400g cans cherry tomatoes
- 1 chicken stock cube
- 1 tbsp balsamic vinegar
- 2 tbsp capers (optional)
- handful of pitted green olives
- 300g orzo , rinsed (to keep it from getting too sticky when baked)

Method

STEP 1

Heat the oven to 220C/200C fan/gas 7. Rub 1 tbsp oil over the chicken and season well, then put skin-side up in an ovenproof casserole dish or roasting tin and bake for 20-25 mins until crisp and golden, but not cooked all the way though. Remove from the dish and put on a plate.

STEP 2

Add the remaining oil to the dish, mixing it with the chicken fat. Tip in the onion and garlic, then bake for 5-8 mins until the onion is tender.

STEP 3

Pour in the wine, stirring it with the onions, then leave to evaporate slightly in the residual heat before adding the bay, thyme, rosemary, parsley stalks and tomatoes. Dissolve the stock cube in 300ml boiling water and pour this in, then add the vinegar, capers, if using, olives and orzo. Stir well and season.

STEP 4

Nestle the chicken back in the pan, skin-side up, and roast for 20 mins until the sauce is thickened, the orzo is tender and the meat is cooked through. Give it a stir, then leave for 10 mins for the orzo to absorb the excess liquid. Scatter over the parsley leaves to serve.

One-pot paneer curry pie

Prep:25 mins **Cook:**1 hr and 30 mins

Serves 6

Ingredients

- 2 tbsp vegetable oil
- 440g paneer , cut into 2cm cubes

- 4 tbsp ghee or butter
- 2 large onions , finely sliced
- 2 large garlic cloves , crushed
- thumb-sized piece of ginger , finely grated
- ½ tsp hot chilli powder
- 2 tsp ground cumin
- 2 tsp fenugreek seeds
- 1½ tbsp garam masala
- 2 x 400g cans chopped tomatoes
- 1 tbsp caster sugar
- 300g potato , peeled and cut into 2cm cubes
- 150g spinach
- 150g frozen peas
- 100ml double cream
- 2 tbsp cashew nut butter
- plain flour , for dusting
- 320g sheet all-butter puff pastry
- 2 large eggs , 1 whole, 1 yolk only, lightly beaten together (freeze the leftover egg white for another recipe)
- 2 tsp nigella seeds
- pilau rice or green veg, to serve

Method

STEP 1

Heat the oil over a medium heat in a shallow flameproof casserole dish roughly 30cm wide. Add the paneer and fry for 5 mins, turning with tongs until each side is golden. Remove from the pan and set aside on a plate lined with kitchen paper.

STEP 2

Heat the ghee or butter in the same dish over a medium-low heat, then add the onions and a big pinch of salt. Fry for 15 mins, or until softened and caramelised. Stir in the garlic and ginger, cook for 1 min, then tip in the spices and fry for a further 2 mins. Scrape the spiced onions into a food processor or blender along with the tomatoes and blitz until smooth. Pour back into the pan with 1½ cans of water, then stir through the sugar and potatoes. Bring to the boil, lower to a simmer, then cover and cook, stirring occasionally, for 20-25 mins or until the potato is just tender.

STEP 3

Add the spinach and peas, and cook for 5 mins. Stir in the cream and cashew butter, then return the paneer to the pan and season to taste. Remove from the heat and set aside to cool completely.

STEP 4

Heat the oven to 220C/200C fan/gas 8. On a lightly floured surface, roll the pastry out to just bigger than your casserole dish. Cut a thin strip off each side and fix these around the edge of the casserole. Roll the pastry sheet over the top and press the edges with a fork to seal, and tuck in any overhang. Brush with the egg, sprinkle with the nigella seeds and bake for 30-35 mins or until deep golden brown. Leave to rest for 15 mins before serving with pilau rice or green veg.

Hearty lentil one pot

Prep:10 mins **Cook:**1 hr

Serves 4

Ingredients

- 40g dried porcini mushrooms , roughly chopped
- 200g dried brown lentils
- 1 ½ tbsp chopped rosemary
- 3 tbsp rapeseed oil
- 2 large onions , roughly chopped
- 150g chestnut baby button mushrooms

- 4 garlic cloves , finely grated
- 2 tbsp vegetable bouillon powder
- 2 large carrots (350g), cut into chunks
- 3 celery sticks (165g), chopped
- 500g potatoes , cut into chunks
- 200g cavolo nero , shredded

Method

STEP 1

Cover the mushrooms in boiling water and leave to soak for 10 mins. Boil the lentils in a pan with plenty of water for 10 mins. Drain and rinse, then tip into a pan with the dried mushrooms and soaking water (don't add the last bit of the liquid as it can contain some grit), rosemary and 2 litres water. Season, cover and simmer for 20 mins.

STEP 2

Meanwhile, heat the oil in a large pan and fry the onions for 5 mins. Stir in the fresh mushrooms and garlic and fry for 5 mins more. Stir in the lentil mixture and bouillon powder, then add the carrots, celery and potatoes. Cover and cook for 20 mins, stirring often, until the veg and lentils are tender, topping up the water level if needed.

STEP 3

Remove any tough stalks from the cavolo nero, then add to the pan and cover and cook for 5 mins more. If you're following our Healthy Diet Plan, serve half in bowls, then chill the rest to eat another day. *Will keep in the fridge for two to three days.* Reheat in a pan until hot.

Lemony tuna, tomato & caper one-pot pasta

Prep:5 mins **Cook:**30 mins

Serves 4

Ingredients

- 2 tbsp olive oil
- 1 red onion , finely chopped
- 500g cherry tomatoes , halved
- 400g dried pasta (we used rigatoni)
- 1l hot vegetable stock
- 2 x 110g cans tuna in olive oil, drained

- 3 tbsp mascarpone
- 30g parmesan , grated
- 2 heaped tbsp capers
- ½ lemon , zested
- small bunch parsley , finely chopped

Method

STEP 1

Heat the oil in a saucepan over a medium-low heat. Add the onion and a pinch of salt and fry gently for 7 mins or until softened and turning translucent. Add 350g of the tomatoes, the pasta and veg stock to the pan and bring to the boil, then reduce to a simmer and cook for 15 mins, uncovered, stirring occasionally. The tomatoes should have broken down and the pasta will be just cooked.

STEP 2

Add the remaining tomatoes and bubble uncovered on a medium-high heat for 5 mins or until the liquid has reduced. Gently fold through large flakes of tuna, the mascarpone, parmesan, capers, lemon zest and parsley as well as salt and a generous grind of black pepper. Place a lid on the pan and leave to sit for 5 mins before serving in deep bowls.

Tomato, pepper & bean one pot

Prep:15 mins **Cook:**45 mins

Makes 6 portions

Ingredients

- 1 tbsp olive oil
- 1 large onion , finely chopped
- 2 celery sticks , finely chopped
- 3 carrots , finely chopped
- 3 red peppers , sliced
- 2 garlic cloves , crushed
- 2 tbsp tomato purée
- 400g can cannellini beans , rinsed and drained
- 400g pinto beans , rinsed and drained
- 400g borlotti beans , rinsed and drained
- 2 x 400g cans chopped tomatoes
- 1 vegetable stock cube (check the label if you're vegan)
- 2 bay leaves
- 1 tbsp brown sugar
- ½ tbsp red wine vinegar

Method

STEP 1

Heat the oil in a large pan or casserole on a medium heat. Fry the onion, celery and carrots for 10 mins until soft and golden, then add the peppers and fry for another 5 mins.

STEP 2

Stir in the garlic for a minute, then add the tomato purée, all the beans and chopped tomatoes, then swirl out the tomato cans with a splash of water and add to the pan with the stock cube, bay leaves, sugar and vinegar. Season and simmer, uncovered, for 25 mins until the sauce reduces to coat the beans and the peppers are soft. Leave to cool before storing in transportable containers. *Will keep in the fridge for 3 - 4 days or freeze in portions and defrost in the fridge overnight.*

Choose your toppings

Sweet & spicy
Add diced dried apricots and 1 tbsp harissa. Top with yogurt swirled with more harissa, and toasted flaked almonds.

Tex-Mex
Stir in ½ - 1 tbsp chipotle paste, shredded leftover roast chicken if you have any, and top with diced avocado, grated cheddar and coriander.

Smoky BBQ beans
Stir in 1 tbsp smoky BBQ sauce and crumble over shop-bought crispy bacon, a dollop of soured cream or yogurt, and some chopped herbs.

Added greens

Stir in some spinach and top with a sliced boiled egg.

Beans on toast

Serve the beans on toast or bread, add a dash of Tabasco or chilli flakes, crumble over feta and drizzle with olive oil.

Italian-inspired

Top with toasted croutons, chopped rosemary, lemon zest and parmesan.

One-pot coconut fish curry

Prep: 5 mins **Cook:** 25 mins

Serves 4

Ingredients

- 1 tbsp sunflower oil , vegetable oil or coconut oil
- 1 onion , chopped
- 1 large garlic clove , crushed
- 1 tsp turmeric
- 1 tsp garam masala

- 1 tsp chilli flakes
- 400ml can coconut milk
- 390g pack fish pie mix
- 200g frozen peas
- 1 lime , cut into wedges
- yogurt and rice, to serve

Method

STEP 1

Heat the oil in a large saucepan over a medium heat, add the onion and a big pinch of salt. Gently fry until the onion is translucent, so around 10 mins, then add the garlic and spices. Stir and cook for another minute, adding a splash of water to prevent them sticking. Tip in the coconut milk and stir well, then simmer for 10 mins.

STEP 2

Tip the fish pie mix and the frozen peas into the pan and cook until the peas are bright green and the fish is starting the flake, so around 3 mins. Season and add lime juice to taste. Ladle into bowls and serve with yogurt and rice.

One-pot chicken & mushroom risotto

Prep:15 mins **Cook:**35 mins

Serves 4

Ingredients

- 60g butter
- 1 large onion, finely chopped
- 2 thyme sprigs, leaves picked
- 250g pack chestnut mushrooms, sliced
- 300g risotto rice
- 1½l hot chicken stock

- 200g cooked chicken, chopped into chunks
- 50g grated parmesan, plus extra to serve (optional)
- small pack parsley, finely chopped

Method

STEP 1

Heat the butter in a large pan over a gentle heat and add the onion. Cook for 10 mins until softened, then stir in the thyme leaves and mushrooms. Cook for 5 mins, sprinkle in the rice and stir to coat in the mixture.

STEP 2

Ladle in a quarter of the stock and continue cooking, stirring occasionally and topping up with more stock as it absorbs (you may not need all the stock).

STEP 3

When most of the stock has been absorbed and the rice is nearly cooked, add the chicken and stir to warm through. Season well and stir in the parmesan and parsley. Serve scattered with extra parmesan, if you like.

Sausage, roasted veg & Puy lentil one-pot

Prep:5 mins **Cook:**45 mins

Serves 4

Ingredients

- 8 sausages
- 2 x 400g packs ready-to-roast vegetables
- 3 garlic cloves , bashed in their skins
- 2 tbsp olive oil
- 1 tsp smoked paprika
- 2 x 250g pouches puy lentils
- 1 ½ tbsp sherry or red wine vinegar
- 1 small pack parsley , roughly chopped

Method

STEP 1

Heat grill to high. Put the sausages in a large roasting tin and grill for 8-10 mins until browning, then switch the oven on to 200C/180C fan/gas 6. Remove the tin from the oven and add the vegetables and garlic, then drizzle over the oil and toss in the paprika and some seasoning.

STEP 2

Roast for 30-35 mins more until the sausages and veg are mostly tender, then stir through the lentils and vinegar. Return to the oven for 5 mins until everything is heated through. Squeeze the garlic cloves out of their skins and stir the garlic into the lentils, then season to taste, stir through the parsley and serve.

Moroccan chicken one-pot

Prep:20 mins **Cook:**50 mins

Serves 6

Ingredients

- 4 boneless, skinless chicken breasts
- 3 tbsp olive oil
- 2 onions, 1 roughly chopped, 1 sliced
- 100g tomatoes
- 100g ginger, roughly chopped
- 3 garlic cloves
- 1 tsp turmeric
- 1 tbsp each ground cumin, coriander and cinnamon
- 1 large butternut squash, deseeded and cut into big chunks
- 600ml chicken stock
- 2 tbsp brown sugar
- 2 tbsp red wine vinegar
- 100g dried cherries

To serve

- 1 small red onion, finely chopped
- zest 1 lemon
- handful mint leaves
- 100g feta cheese, crumbled

- couscous and natural yogurt

Method

STEP 1

Season 4 boneless, skinless chicken breasts. Heat 2 tbsp olive oil in a flameproof dish, then brown the chicken on all sides. Remove the chicken to a plate.

STEP 2

Whizz 1 chopped onion, 100g tomatoes, 100g chopped ginger and 3 garlic cloves into a rough paste.

STEP 3

Fry 1 sliced onion in 1 tbsp olive oil in the dish until softened, then add 1 tsp turmeric, 1 tbsp cumin, 1 tbsp coriander and 1 tbsp cinnamon and fry for 1 min more until fragrant. Add the paste and fry for another few mins to soften.

STEP 4

Return the chicken to the dish with 1 large butternut squash, cut into big chunks, 600ml chicken stock, 2 tbsp brown sugar and 2 tbsp red wine vinegar.

STEP 5

Bring to a simmer, then cook for 30 mins until the chicken is cooked through.

STEP 6

Lift the chicken out and stir in 100g dried cherries, then continue simmering the sauce to thicken while you shred the chicken into bite-sized chunks. Stir the chicken back into the sauce and season.

STEP 7

Mix 1 finely chopped small red onion, the zest of 1 lemon, a handful of mint leaves and 100g crumbled feta cheese. Scatter over the dish, then serve with couscous and natural yogurt.

One-pot Chinese chicken noodle soup

Prep: 10 mins **Cook:** 15 mins

Serves 4

Ingredients

- 1 tbsp honey
- 3 tbsp dark soy
- 1 red chilli , sliced
- 1l chicken stock
- 80g leftover roast chicken (optional)
- 20g pickled pink ginger or normal ginger, peeled and finely sliced
- ½ Chinese cabbage , shredded
- 300g pouch straight-to-wok thick noodles
- 4 spring onions , sliced

Method

STEP 1

Drizzle the honey over the base of a large saucepan and bubble briefly to a caramel, then splash in the soy, bubble, add half the chilli and the chicken stock and simmer for 5 mins.

STEP 2

Add the chicken, if using, and ginger, and simmer for another 5 mins. Stir in the cabbage and noodles and cook until just wilted and the noodles have heated through. Ladle into bowls and sprinkle over the remaining chilli and the spring onions.

Spring one-pot roast chicken

Prep:20 mins **Cook:**1 hr and 20 mins

Serves 4

Ingredients

- 1 ½kg whole chicken
- 250g mascarpone
- ½ small lemon , zested and juiced
- small bunch of tarragon , finely chopped
- 3 tbsp olive oil
- 800g new potatoes , halved if large
- 1 garlic bulb , halved
- 200g radishes , halved if large
- ½ bunch of spring onions , trimmed
- 150ml chicken stock
- 200g frozen peas , defrosted
- 100g spring greens , shredded

Method

STEP 1

Heat the oven to 200C/180C fan/gas 6. Remove any string from the chicken and sit in a large roasting tin or a baking dish, with plenty of space around it.

STEP 2

Mash 2 tbsp of the mascarpone with the lemon zest, 1 tbsp of the tarragon and some seasoning. Slip your hand beneath the chicken skin to pull it away from the meat, then spread the mixture beneath the skin in a thin layer. Spoon another 3 tbsp mascarpone into the cavity of the chicken, to melt in with the roasting juices and enrich the sauce later on. Rub 2 tbsp olive oil into the skin, season well with sea salt, then loosely tie the legs together with butcher's string. Roast for 20 mins.

STEP 3

Aarrange the potatoes and the garlic around the chicken, drizzle over another 1 tbsp oil and cook for another 30 mins.

STEP 4

Toss the radishes and whole spring onions into the dish, in and around the potatoes, coating everything in the fat, then roast for another 25 mins. The potatoes and radishes will be golden and tender, and the chicken should be cooked through. Remove the chicken from the tin, cover loosely with foil and leave to rest.

STEP 5

Pour off or spoon away the excess oil from the tin. Stir the remaining mascarpone (about 150g) with the stock in a jug until lump-free, then pour into the tin and bubble on the hob for few minutes, stirring to coat the potatoes and veg. Squeeze over some lemon juice and season.

STEP 6

Stir in the peas, spring greens and most of the remaining tarragon, and bubble for a few more minutes until bright green. Sit the chicken back in the middle of the tin to serve and scatter over the reserved tarragon.

Chicken nacho one-pot

Prep:5 mins **Cook:**20 mins

Serves 4

Ingredients

- 2 tbsp olive oil
- 100g chorizo or pepperoni, skin removed, cut into chunks
- 1 tsp paprika
- 20 cherry tomatoes , cut in half

- 4 skinless chicken breasts , each cut lengthways into 4 (or buy chicken fillets)
- 200g bag corn chips (spicy if you like a bit of heat)
- 200ml tub crème fraîche

To serve

- jar of jalapeño peppers
- extra crème fraîche or soured cream

- smashed avocado

Method

STEP 1

Heat oven to 180C/160C fan/gas 4. Put the oil and chorizo in an ovenproof frying pan over a high heat and cook for 3 mins until the chorizo has released its oils and is starting to crisp. Stir in the paprika and tomatoes, and cook for 1 min.

STEP 2

Season the chicken, add to the pan and cook for 5 mins, keeping the heat high. Add 2 tbsp water so there is a little sauce and the tomatoes cook down a little. Tip into a bowl.

STEP 3

Put the corn chips in the pan and pour the chicken mix on top. Spoon over the crème fraîche and cook in the oven for 10 mins. Serve with the jalapeños, extra crème fraîche or soured cream, and smashed avocado.

Chicken & couscous one-pot

Prep: 10 mins **Cook:** 1 hr

Serves 4

Ingredients

- 8 skin on, bone-in chicken thighs
- 2 tsp turmeric
- 1 tbsp garam masala
- 2 tbsp sunflower oil
- 2 onions, finely sliced
- 3 garlic cloves, sliced
- 500ml chicken stock (from a cube is fine)
- large handful whole green olives
- zest and juice 1 lemon
- 250g couscous
- small bunch flat-leaf parsley, chopped

Method

STEP 1

Toss the chicken thighs in half the spices and a pinch of salt until completely coated. Heat 1 tbsp oil in a large sauté pan with a lid. Fry chicken, skin-side down, for 10 mins until golden brown, turn over, then cook for 2 mins before removing from the pan. Pour the rest of the oil into the pan, then fry the onions and garlic for 8 mins until golden. Stir in the rest of the spices, then cook for 1 min longer. Pour over the chicken stock and scatter in the olives. Bring everything to the boil, turn down the heat, then sit the chicken, skinside up, in the stock.

STEP 2

Cover the pan with a lid, then simmer gently for 35-40 mins until the chicken is tender. Put the kettle on, then lift the chicken onto a plate and keep warm. Take the pan off the heat. Stir the lemon juice and couscous into the saucy onions in the pan and top up with enough boiling water just to cover the couscous if you need to. Place the lid back on the pan, then leave to stand for 5 mins until the couscous is cooked through. Fluff through half the parsley and the lemon zest, then sit the chicken on top. Scatter with the rest of the parsley and zest before serving.

One-pot chicken chasseur

Prep: 20 mins **Cook:** 1 hr and 30 mins

Serves 4

Ingredients

- 1 tsp olive oil
- 25g butter
- 4 chicken legs
- 1 onion, chopped
- 2 garlic cloves, crushed

- 200g pack small button or chestnut mushrooms
- 225ml red wine
- 2 tbsp tomato purée
- 2 thyme sprigs
- 500ml chicken stock

Method

STEP 1

Heat 1 tsp olive oil and half of the 25g butter in a large lidded casserole.

STEP 2

Season 4 chicken legs, then fry for about 5 mins on each side until golden brown. Remove and set aside.

STEP 3

Melt the remaining butter in the pan. Add 1 chopped onion, then fry for about 5 mins until soft.

STEP 4

Add 2 crushed garlic cloves, cook for about 1 min, add 200g small button or chestnut mushrooms, cook for 2 mins, then add 225ml red wine.

STEP 5

Stir in 2 tbsp tomato purée, let the liquid bubble and reduce for about 5 mins, then stir in 2 thyme sprigs and pour over 500ml chicken stock.

STEP 6

Slip the chicken legs back into the pan, then cover and simmer on a low heat for about 1 hr until the chicken is very tender.

STEP 7

Remove the chicken legs from the pan and keep warm. Rapidly boil down the sauce for 10 mins or so until it is syrupy and the flavour has concentrated.

STEP 8

Put the chicken legs back into the sauce and serve.

One-pot poached spring chicken

Prep: 25 mins **Cook:** 2 hrs and 10 mins

Serves 5 - 6

Ingredients

- 100g butter
- 1 large chicken , about 2kg
- 15 Jersey Royal potatoes , scrubbed and halved
- 100g smoked bacon or pancetta lardons
- 1 thyme sprig
- 6 white peppercorns
- 3 bay leaves
- 250g carrots , tops cut off, halved lengthways
- 200g bunch small turnips , peeled and halved
- 150g podded peas
- 150g podded and peeled broad beans
- 8 spring onions , topped and tailed, then cut into 2cm lengths
- 8 asparagus spears , trimmed
- small handful parsley leaves, chopped
- 1 small tarragon sprig, leaves picked
- 1 lemon , cut in to wedges, to serve

Method

STEP 1

Melt the butter in a small pan, discard the milky liquid, then pour the golden fat into a bowl and set aside – this is clarified butter. Heat oven to 150C/130C fan/gas 2. Sit the chicken in a large flameproof casserole dish, breast-side up, and arrange the potatoes and bacon around it. Pour over 1 litre of water. Add the thyme, pepper and bay, drizzle over the clarified butter and season everything with sea salt. Transfer the dish to the hob and heat until the liquid is starting to simmer. Cover the dish, cook in the oven for 1 hr 15 mins, then add the carrots and turnips. Pop the lid back on and put it back in the oven for another 35 mins.

STEP 2

Scatter the peas, broad beans, onions and asparagus around the chicken, submerging them in the liquid, then cover and return to the oven for a further 10-15 mins or until the vegetables are just cooked.

STEP 3

Remove from the oven, leave to stand for 5 mins, then carefully lift the chicken from the broth onto a board. If you want to crisp up the skin, blast it with a blowtorch. Stir the parsley and tarragon through the broth. Serve in the middle of the table with the vegetables and broth, and offer lemon wedges for squeezing over.

One-pot crystal chicken

Prep:15 mins **Cook:**20 mins

plus 1 hr cooling

Serves 6

Ingredients

- 1 chicken , about 1.5kg (the best quality you can get)
- bunch spring onions , green and white parts separated (keep the whites for ginger & chilli oil, see goes well with)
- 2 thumb-sized pieces ginger , sliced
- small pack coriander , leaves and stalks separated

- 3 garlic cloves , peeled and left whole
- 1 star anise
- 500ml chicken stock , or a chicken stock cube
- 200ml Chinese rice wine or dry sherry
- 4 tbsp soy sauce
- cooked rice and Sichuan pepper, to serve

Method

STEP 1

Put the chicken in a saucepan or stock pot large enough to fit it comfortably. Add the green spring onion parts, ginger, coriander stalks, garlic and star anise. Pour over the stock (or crumble in the stock cube), rice wine and 3 tbsp of the soy sauce, then top up with water to just cover.

STEP 2

Bring everything to the boil and skim once. Turn down to a gentle simmer and poach for 20 mins, then turn off the heat and leave the chicken to cool in the broth for at least 1 hr. This can be done a day ahead but musn't be chilled, otherwise the chicken will be too cold. Remove the chicken from the broth and leave to cool completely, then strain the broth, ready to pour some over the rice later.

STEP 3

To serve, carve the chicken as if you were jointing it. Arrange on a platter, drizzle over the remaining soy and scatter over the coriander leaves and Sichuan pepper. Serve with rice, ginger and chilli oil, and some of the heated broth to moisten the rice. Any leftover broth can be frozen.

One-pot chicken with chorizo & new potatoes

Prep: 15 mins **Cook:** 1 hr and 40 mins

Serves 4

Ingredients

- 1 whole chicken (about 1.5kg), the best quality you can afford
- small knob of butter
- 1 tbsp olive oil
- ½ lemon
- 1 bay leaf
- 1 thyme sprig

- 300g chorizo ring, thickly sliced
- 700g new potatoes , halved (or quartered if really large)
- 12 garlic cloves , left whole and unpeeled
- large splash of dry sherry
- 150ml chicken stock
- handful parsley leaves, roughly chopped

Method

STEP 1

Heat oven to 180C/160C fan/gas 4 and season the chicken all over. In a large flameproof casserole dish with a lid, heat the butter and oil until sizzling, then spend a good 15 mins slowly browning the chicken well all over. Remove from the dish and pop the lemon, bay and thyme in the cavity. Set aside.

STEP 2

Pour most of the oil out of the dish, place back on the heat and sizzle the chorizo for 5 mins until it starts to release its red oil. Throw in the potatoes, sizzle them until they start to colour, then add the garlic. Splash in the sherry, let it bubble down a little, then pour in the stock.

STEP 3

Nestle the chicken, breast-side up, among the potatoes, place the lid on the dish and cook in the oven for 1 hr 15 mins or until the legs easily come away from the body. Leave the chicken to rest for 10 mins, then scatter with parsley and serve straight from the dish.

Easy one-pot chicken casserole

Prep:5 mins **Cook:**50 mins

Serves 4

Ingredients

- 8 bone-in chicken thighs, skin pulled off and discarded
- 1 tbsp oil
- 5 spring onions, sliced
- 2 tbsp plain flour
- 2 chicken stock cubes
- 2 large carrots, cut into batons (no need to peel)
- 400g new potato, halved if large
- 200g frozen peas
- 1 tbsp grainy mustard
- small handful fresh soft herbs, like parsley, chives, dill or tarragon, chopped

Method

STEP 1

Put the kettle on. Fry 8 bone-in chicken thighs in 1 tbsp oil in a casserole dish or wide pan with a lid to quickly brown.

STEP 2

Stir in the whites of 5 spring onions with 2 tbsp plain flour and 2 chicken stock cubes until the flour disappears, then gradually stir in 750ml hot water from the kettle.

STEP 3

Throw in 2 large carrots, in batons and 400g new potatoes, bring to a simmer. Cover and cook for 20 mins.

STEP 4

Take off the lid and simmer for 15 mins more, then throw in 200g peas for another 5 mins.

STEP 5

Season, stir in 1 tbsp grainy mustard, the green spring onion bits, a small handful of fresh soft herbs and some seasoning.

One-pot chicken with quinoa

Prep:5 mins **Cook:**30 mins

Serves 2

Ingredients

- 1 tbsp cold-pressed rapeseed oil
- 2 skinless chicken breasts (about 300g/11oz)
- 1 medium onion , sliced into 12 wedges
- 1 red pepper , deseeded and sliced
- 2 garlic cloves , finely chopped
- 100g green beans , trimmed and cut in half
- 1/4-1/2 tsp chilli flakes , according to taste
- 2 tsp ground cumin
- 2 tsp ground coriander
- 100g uncooked quinoa
- 85g frozen sweetcorn
- 75g kale , thickly shredded

Method

STEP 1

Heat the oil in a large, deep frying pan or sauté pan. Season the chicken and fry over a medium-high heat for 2-3 mins each side or until golden. Transfer to a plate. Add the onion and pepper to the pan and cook for 3 mins, stirring, until softened and lightly browned.

STEP 2

Tip in the garlic and beans, and stir-fry for 2 mins. Add the chilli and spices, then stir in the quinoa and sweetcorn. Pour in 700ml just-boiled water with 1/2 tsp flaked sea salt and bring to the boil.

STEP 3

Return the chicken to the pan, reduce the heat to a simmer and cook for 12 mins, stirring regularly and turning the chicken occasionally. Add the kale and cook for a further 3 mins or until the quinoa and chicken are cooked through.

Spicy sausage & bean one-pot

Prep:5 mins **Cook:**20 mins

Serves 4

Ingredients

- 1 tbsp vegetable oil
- 1 onion , thickly sliced
- 8 Cumberland sausages
- 1 fat garlic clove , crushed

- 2 x 400g cans kidney beans in chilli sauce
- 2-3 sprigs curly parsley , chopped

Method

STEP 1

Heat the oil in a large frying pan. Cook the onion and sausages over a fairly high heat for 8-10 mins, turning the sausages often so they brown all over.

STEP 2

Add the garlic to the pan with the kidney beans and their sauce. Half-fill one of the cans with water, swirl and then add this to the pan. Stir everything together and bring to the boil. Turn down to simmer and cook for 10 mins, or until the sausages are cooked through. Season and sprinkle with the parsley.

Spring chicken one-pot

Prep:10 mins **Cook:**55 mins

Serves 4

Ingredients

- 1 tbsp olive oil

- 8 chicken thighs , skin on and bone in

- 1 onion , sliced
- 200g streaky bacon , chopped
- 1 carrot , chopped
- 2 large spring greens , shredded
- 600ml chicken stock
- 300g baby new potato
- 2 tbsp crème fraîche
- 2 tbsp basil pesto
- crusty bread , to serve (optional)

Method

STEP 1

Heat the oil in a large, heavy-based pan with a lid. Season the chicken and brown all over. Remove the chicken to a plate and cook the onion and bacon for 5 mins until softened and lightly coloured.

STEP 2

Return the chicken to the pan, and add the remaining ingredients, except the crème fraîche and pesto, along with plenty of freshly ground black pepper. Bring to the boil, then cover and gently simmer for 30-40 mins until the potatoes are tender and chicken cooked through.

STEP 3

Stir in the crème fraîche and pesto. Serve with some crusty bread for mopping up the sauce, if you like.

One-pot mushroom & potato curry

Prep:10 mins **Cook:**20 mins

Serves 4

Ingredients

1 tbsp oil

1 onion, roughly chopped

1 large potato, chopped into small chunks

1 aubergine, trimmed and chopped into chunks

250g button mushrooms

2-4 tbsp curry paste (depending on how hot you like it)

150ml vegetable stock

400ml can reduced-fat coconut milk

chopped coriander, to serve

Method

STEP 1

Heat the oil in a large saucepan, add the onion and potato. Cover, then cook over a low heat for 5 mins until the potatoes start to soften. Throw in the aubergine and mushrooms, then cook for a few more mins.

STEP 2

Stir in the curry paste, pour over the stock and coconut milk. Bring to the boil, then simmer for 10 mins or until the potato is tender. Stir through the coriander and serve with rice or naan bread.

Smoky pork & Boston beans one-pot

Prep:15 mins **Cook:**40 mins

Serves 4

Ingredients

- 2 tbsp olive oil
- 2 garlic cloves , crushed
- 2 tbsp smoked paprika
- 500g pork loin steaks , quartered
- 2 x 400g cans cannellini beans , drained and rinsed
- 400g passata

- 2 tsp chipotle paste
- 1 tbsp dark soft brown sugar
- 100g ham hock , in large shreds
- 4 slices crusty white bread
- small handful flat-leaf parsley , roughly chopped

Method

STEP 1

Heat oven to 180C/160C fan/gas 4. Mix the oil, garlic and paprika together and rub into the pork. In a large, shallow ovenproof dish, mix the cannellini beans, passata, chipotle, sugar and ham hock. Nestle the pork into the beans. Bake in the oven for 40 mins until the pork is cooked through.

STEP 2

Toast the bread and serve on the side. Sprinkle the parsley over the pork and beans to serve.

Chilli chicken one-pot

Prep: 20 mins **Cook:** 1 hr and 5 mins

Serves 8

Ingredients

- 2 large onions, halved and sliced
- 2 tbsp olive oil
- 265g chorizo ring, peeled and thickly sliced
- 4 red peppers, deseeded and cut into large chunks
- 2 x 400g/14oz can chopped tomato

To serve

- 15g pack coriander, chopped
- 2-3 avocado, skinned and sliced

- 2 chicken stock cubes
- ½-1 tsp dried chilli flakes
- 2 tsp dried oregano
- 16 boneless skinless chicken thighs
- 3 x 410g/14oz cans red kidney beans, drained

- good squeeze lime juice

Method

STEP 1

Heat oven to 180C/fan 160C/gas 4. Fry the onions in the oil for 5 mins until they become soft and start to colour. Add the chorizo and fry for a few mins more. Stir in the peppers, then pour in the tomatoes, followed by a can of water, the stock cubes, chilli and oregano.

STEP 2

Arrange the chicken thighs on top of the sauce, pushing them under the liquid. Bring to a simmer, cover, then cook in the oven for 40 mins. Add the beans, stir, then cook for 20 mins more. You can make this up to 2 days ahead and keep chilled.

STEP 3

31

To serve, reheat on the top of the stove or in the oven at 190C/fan 170C/gas 5 for 1 hr 10 mins until piping hot. Stir in most of the coriander, toss the rest with the avocado, lime and a little salt, then pile this on top. Serve with Garlic & oregano bread (below) and a bag of green salad tossed with olives, cherry tomatoes and finely sliced red onion.

Chinese-style braised beef one-pot

Prep: 10 mins **Cook:** 2 hrs - 2 hrs and 30 mins

Serves 6

Ingredients

- 3-4 tbsp olive oil
- 6 garlic cloves, thinly sliced
- good thumb-size piece fresh root ginger, peeled and shredded
- 1 bunch spring onions, sliced
- 1 red chilli, deseeded and thinly sliced
- 1 ½kg braising beef, cut into large pieces (we used ox cheek)
- 2 tbsp plain flour, well seasoned

- 1 tsp Chinese five-spice powder
- 2 star anise (optional)
- 2 tsp light muscovado sugar (or use whatever you've got)
- 3 tbsp Chinese cooking wine or dry sherry
- 3 tbsp dark soy sauce, plus more to serve
- 500ml beef stock (we used Knorr Touch of Taste)

steamed bok choi and steamed basmati rice, to serve

Method

STEP 1

Heat 2 tbsp of the oil in a large, shallow casserole. Fry the garlic, ginger, onions and chilli for 3 mins until soft and fragrant. Tip onto a plate. Toss the beef in the flour, add 1 tbsp more oil to the pan, then brown the meat in batches, adding the final tbsp oil if you need to. It should take about 5 mins to brown each batch properly.

STEP 2

Add the five-spice and star anise (if using) to the pan, tip in the gingery mix, then fry for 1 min until the spices are fragrant. Add the sugar, then the beef and stir until combined. Keep the heat high, then splash in the wine or sherry, scraping up any meaty bits. Heat oven to 150C/fan 130C/gas 2.

STEP 3

Pour in the soy and stock (it won't cover the meat completely), bring to a simmer, then tightly cover, transfer to the oven and cook for 1½-2 hrs, stirring the meat halfway through. The meat should be very soft, and any sinewy bits should have melted away. Season with more soy. This can now be chilled and frozen for up to 1 month.

STEP 4

Nestle the cooked bok choi into the pan, then bring to the table with the basmati rice straight away and tuck in.

Spanish rice & prawn one-pot

Prep:4 mins **Cook:**16 mins

Serves 4

Ingredients

- 1 onion, sliced
- 1 red and 1 green pepper, deseeded and sliced
- 50g chorizo, sliced
- 2 garlic cloves, crushed
- 1 tbsp olive oil

- 250g easy cook basmati rice (we used Tilda)
- 400g can chopped tomato
- 200g raw, peeled prawns, defrosted if frozen

Method

STEP 1

Boil the kettle. In a non-stick frying or shallow pan with a lid, fry the onion, peppers, chorizo and garlic in the oil over a high heat for 3 mins. Stir in the rice and chopped tomatoes with 500ml boiling water, cover, then cook over a high heat for 12 mins.

STEP 2

Uncover, then stir – the rice should be almost tender. Stir in the prawns, with a splash more water if the rice is looking dry, then cook for another min until the prawns are just pink and rice tender.

Sausage & lentil one-pot

Prep:5 mins **Cook:**40 mins

Serves 4

Ingredients

- 1 tbsp olive oil
- 400g pack sausage
- 1 onion, finely chopped
- 1 garlic clove, crushed

- 1 red pepper, sliced
- 250g lentil (we used puy lentils)
- 150ml vegetable stock
- 125ml red wine or extra stock

Method

STEP 1

Heat oil in a pan, cook the sausages until browned, then remove. Tip in remaining oil, onion, garlic and pepper, then cook, about 5 mins more until softened. Add lentils and sausages to the pan with the stock and wine, if using.

STEP 2

Bring up to the boil, then simmer for 20 mins until lentils have softened and sausages are cooked through. Serve with plenty of crusty bread.

Sausage & veg one-pot

Prep:10 mins **Cook:**55 mins

Serves 4

Ingredients

- 1 tbsp olive oil
- 12 good-quality sausages
- 1 small onion , chopped
- 1 fennel bulb , quartered, then sliced
- 2 garlic cloves , crushed
- ½ red chilli , finely chopped
- 2 tsp fennel seed

- 2 tbsp plain flour
- 150ml white wine
- 500ml chicken stock
- 200g pack green bean , halved
- 300g broad bean , double podded (unpodded weight)
- 300g pea

- 200g pot half-fat crème fraîche
- zest 1 lemon , juice of ½
- handful parsley , chopped
- handful basil , chopped
- ½ red chilli , finely chopped, to serve
- crusty bread , to serve

Method

STEP 1

Heat the oil in a large pan. Add the sausages, cook for a few mins until browned all over, then transfer to a plate. Tip the onion and fennel into the pan and cook for 10-15 mins until nice and soft, then add the garlic, half the chilli and the fennel seeds. Cook for a few mins more, moving everything around the pan now and then, to prevent the garlic from burning.

STEP 2

Stir the flour into the vegetables, and cook for 1 min. Pour in the wine, let it bubble for 1 min, give everything a good stir, then add the stock and return the sausages to the pan, seasoning well. Cover, then gently simmer for 30 mins.

STEP 3

Add the green beans, broad beans and peas, then cook, uncovered, for 2 mins more. Stir in the crème fraîche, lemon zest and juice, and herbs. Add a little more salt and pepper if it needs it, sprinkle with the chilli, then serve with plenty of bread for soaking up the juices.

One-pot Moroccan chicken

Prep:5 mins **Cook:**25 mins

Serves 4

Ingredients

- 4 skinless chicken breasts
- 1 tsp ground cumin
- 1 tbsp olive oil
- 1 onion , finely sliced
- 400g can cherry tomato
- 2 tbsp harissa paste (we used Belazu Rose Harissa)
- 1 tbsp clear honey
- 2 medium courgettes , thickly sliced
- 400g can chickpea , drained and rinsed

Method

STEP 1

Season the chicken breasts all over with the cumin and lots of ground black pepper. Heat the oil in a large non-stick frying pan and cook the chicken with the onion for 4 mins. Turn the chicken over and cook for a further 3 mins. Stir the onions around the chicken regularly as they cook.

STEP 2

Tip the tomatoes and 250ml water into the pan and stir in the harissa, honey, courgettes and chickpeas. Bring to a gentle simmer and cook for 15 mins until the chicken is tender and the sauce has thickened slightly.

Fragrant pork & rice one-pot

Prep:15 mins **Cook:**30 mins

Serves 4

Ingredients

- 4-6 good-quality sausages
- 1 tbsp olive oil
- ½ onion , finely chopped
- 2 garlic cloves , crushed
- 2 tsp each ground cumin and coriander

- 140g long grain rice
- 850ml vegetable stock
- 400g can chopped tomato
- ½ small bunch coriander , leaves picked

Method

STEP 1

Split the sausage skins, squeeze out the meat, then roll it into small meatballs about the size of a large olive. Heat the oil in a large non-stick saucepan, then brown the meatballs well on all sides until cooked – you might need to do this in batches. Set the meatballs aside.

STEP 2

Add the onion and garlic to the pan. Soften for 5 mins, stir in the spices and rice, then cook for another min. Pour in the stock and tomatoes. Bring to a simmer, scraping up any sausagey bits from the bottom of the pan. Simmer for 10 mins until the rice is just cooked, then stir in the meatballs with some seasoning. Ladle into bowls, scatter with coriander and serve with crusty bread.

One-pot partridge with drunken potatoes

Prep:30 mins **Cook:**40 mins

Serves 2

Ingredients

- 2 partridge
- 2 juniper berries , crushed
- 2 thyme sprigs
- 2 bay leaves
- 2 garlic cloves , skin on, bashed
- 4 thin slices smoked streaky bacon
- chopped parsley , to serve
- buttered cavolo nero or shredded sprout tops, to serve
- 2 tbsp duck fat or butter
- 1 large Maris Piper potato (about 300g)
- glass of full-bodied red wine (about 100ml)
- 150ml chicken stock

Method

STEP 1

Season the partridges (including the cavity) generously. Put a juniper berry, a thyme sprig, a bay leaf and a garlic clove in each cavity. Chop the bacon into chunky pieces and slice the potato lengthways into six thick slices, discarding the ends.

STEP 2

Heat oven to 180C/160C fan/gas 4. Heat half the duck fat or butter in a flameproof casserole dish until just sizzling, then brown the birds on all sides for 10 mins. Remove them from the dish and set aside. Add the rest of the fat to the dish and gently fry the potato slices until very brown and crisp on each side. Add the bacon and sizzle with the potatoes until starting to brown. Sit the birds on top of the potatoes and pour over the wine and stock. Put in the oven, uncovered, for 15 mins.

STEP 3

Remove the birds from the dish and leave somewhere warm to rest for 10 mins. Baste the potatoes, return to the oven until cooked through, then scatter over the parsley.

STEP 4

To serve, sit the birds back in the pan and bring to the table or plate up with the potatoes. Serve with cavolo nero or sprout tops.

Chorizo, new potato & haddock one-pot

Prep:10 mins **Cook:**20 mins

Serves 2

Ingredients

- 1 tbsp extra-virgin olive oil , plus extra to serve
- 50g chorizo , peeled and thinly sliced
- 450g salad or new potatoes , sliced (I used Charlotte)

- crusty bread , to serve

- 4 tbsp dry sherry , or more if you need it (or use white wine)
- 2 skinless thick fillets white fish (I used sustainably caught haddock)
- good handful cherry tomatoes , halved
- 20g bunch parsley , chopped

Method

STEP 1

Heat a large lidded frying pan, then add the oil. Tip in the chorizo, fry for 2 mins until it starts to release its oils, then tip in the potatoes and some seasoning. Splash over 3 tbsp sherry, cover the pan tightly, then leave to cook for 10-15 mins until the potatoes are just tender. Move them around the pan a bit halfway through.

STEP 2

Season the fish well. Give the potatoes another stir, add the cherry tomatoes and most of the chopped parsley to the pan, then lay the fish on top. Splash over 1 tbsp sherry, put the lid on again, then leave to cook for 5 mins, or until the fish has turned white and is flaky when prodded in the middle. Scatter the whole dish with a little more parsley and drizzle with more extra virgin oil. Serve straight away with crusty bread.

Summer chicken one-pot

Prep: 10 mins **Cook:** 40 mins

Serves 4

Ingredients

- 8 chicken thighs
- 2 tbsp plain flour
- 1 tbsp olive oil
- 8 rashers streaky bacon , chopped
- 400ml stock
- 500g bag baby new potatoes , halved

- 200g pack full fat soft cheese
- 200g broad beans , podded
- 200g sweetcorn (frozen, fresh or from a can)
- 200g cherry tomatoes , halved

Method

STEP 1

Dust the chicken in the flour and some seasoning. Heat the oil in a lidded pan and brown the chicken, in batches if needed, then transfer to a plate. Throw in the bacon and fry for 5 mins, until crisp.

STEP 2

Return the chicken to the pan. Add the stock, cover and simmer for 30 mins, adding the potatoes after 10 mins.

STEP 3

Make sure the chicken is cooked and the potatoes are tender, then stir in the cheese, the rest of the vegetables and some seasoning. Simmer for 5 mins more, uncovered, then serve.

One-pot chicken pilaf

Prep: 5 mins **Cook:** 20 mins

Serves 1

Ingredients

- 1 tsp sunflower oil

- 1 small onion , chopped

- 1 large or 2 small boneless, skinless chicken thigh fillets, cut into chunks
- 2 tsp curry paste (choose your favourite)
- a third of a mug basmati rice
- two-thirds of a mug chicken stock
- 1 mug frozen mixed vegetables
- half a mug frozen leaf spinach

Method

STEP 1

Heat the oil in a frying pan, then fry the onion for 5-6 mins until softened. Add the chicken pieces, fry for a further couple of mins just to colour the outside, then stir in curry paste and rice. Cook for another min.

STEP 2

Pour in the chicken stock and throw in any larger bits of frozen veg. Bring to the boil, lower the heat, then cover the pan with a lid. Cook for 10 mins, then stir in the remaining veg. Scatter over the spinach, cover, then cook for 10 mins more until all the stock is absorbed and the rice is tender. Give everything a good stir, season to taste, then tuck in.

One-pot chicken & bacon stew

Prep:20 mins **Cook:**1 hr and 30 mins

Serves 8

Ingredients

- 3 tbsp olive oil
- 16 chicken pieces on the bone (about 3kg/6lb 8oz in total)
- 140g smoked bacon, chopped or lardons or cubetti di pancetta
- 4 medium carrots, thickly sliced
- 2 onions, roughly chopped
- 2 tbsp plain flour
- 1 tbsp tomato purée
- 75ml white wine or cider vinegar
- 1l chicken stock
- 2 bay leaves
- 4 tbsp double cream or crème fraîche
- 600g small new potatoes, halved
- 12 large white mushrooms, quartered
- chopped herbs, such as parsley, tarragon or chives

Method

STEP 1

Heat oven to 200C/180C fan/gas 6. Heat the oil in a large flameproof casserole with a lid. Fry the chicken pieces in batches for 5 mins on each side until well browned, then transfer to a plate. Sizzle the bacon in the casserole for a few mins until beginning to crisp. Stir in the carrots and onions, then cook for 5 mins until starting to soften. Stir in the flour and tomato purée and cook for 1 min more. Finally, splash in the vinegar and stir well.

STEP 2

Pour in the stock and bring to a simmer. Add the bay, cream and seasoning. Slide in the chicken pieces and scatter over the potatoes, turning everything over a few times so that the potatoes are immersed in the sauce. Put the lid on and place in the oven. After 40 mins, remove from the oven and stir in the mushrooms. Cover again and cook in the oven for 10 mins more until the chicken is cooked through and tender but not completely falling off the bone. You can now turn off the heat, and chill and freeze some or all of it (see freezing tips, below). If eating straight away, cook for 10 mins more, then sprinkle over the herbs and serve.

Squash, chicken & couscous one-pot

Prep: 15 mins **Cook:** 45 mins

Serves 4

Ingredients

- 2 tbsp harissa paste
- 1 tsp each ground cumin and ground coriander
- 2 red onions , halved and cut into thin wedges
- 2 skinless chicken breasts , cut into bite-sized chunks

- 1 small butternut squash , cut into 1cm chunks (no need to peel)
- x cans tomatoes
- zest and juice 2 lemons
- 200g cherry tomato , halved
- 140g couscous
- small bunch coriander , roughly chopped

Method

STEP 1

Heat a large non-stick casserole dish or pan on the hob. Add the harissa, spices and onions, stir and cook gently for 10 mins until soft. Add chicken and brown for 5-10 mins. Add squash, stirring to combine, and a splash of water if it starts to stick. Cook for 5 mins more.

STEP 2

Tip canned tomatoes into the pan with ½ can of water, cover and simmer for 20-30 mins. Add the lemon zest and juice, cherry tomatoes, couscous and seasoning. Cover and turn off the heat. Leave on the hob for 10 mins, then stir through the coriander and serve.

Mushroom & rice one-pot

Prep:20 mins **Cook:**30 mins

Serves 4

Ingredients

- 200g basmati rice
- 1 tbsp olive oil
- 1 large onion , chopped
- 2 tsp chopped rosemary or 1 tsp dried
- 250g chestnut mushroom , quartered

- 2 red peppers , sliced
- 400g can chopped tomato
- 425ml vegetable stock
- handful parsley , chopped

Method

STEP 1

Heat oven to 190C/fan 170C/gas 5. Tip the rice into a sieve, rinse under cold running water, then leave to drain. Heat the oil in a flameproof casserole, add the onion, then fry until softened, about 5 mins. Stir in the rosemary and mushrooms, then fry briefly. Add the rice, stir to coat in the oil, then add the peppers, tomatoes, stock and some freshly ground pepper. Bring to the boil, give it a stir, cover tightly with a lid, then bake for 20-25 mins until the rice is tender. Scatter over the parsley and serve.

One-pot pork with orange, olives & bay

Prep:35 mins **Cook:**2 hrs and 40 mins

Serves 6

Ingredients

- 85g sundried tomato in oil, roughly chopped, plus 2-3 tbsp oil from the jar
- 1kg pork shoulder , cut into chunky cubes

- 2 tbsp plain flour , seasoned
- 400g shallot (see tip, below)
- 1 onion , thinly sliced

- 3 bay leaves
- few thyme sprigs
- 5 garlic cloves , thinly sliced
- 400ml red wine
- strip of zest and juice from 1 orange
- 350ml chicken stock
- 400g can chopped plum tomato
- 800g large new potato , peeled & halved or cut into fat slices, depending on size
- 70g pack dry black olive

Method

STEP 1

Heat 1 tbsp of the sundried tomato oil in a large, flameproof casserole dish. Toss the pork in the flour, tap off any excess, then brown it in 2 batches, transferring to a large bowl once golden and crusted. Use a splash more oil for the second batch if needed.

STEP 2

Tip 1 tbsp oil, shallots, onion, bay leaves and thyme into the pan and fry for 5 mins until golden here and there. Stir in the garlic and sundried tomatoes, cook for 1 min more, then tip onto the pork.

STEP 3

Splash the wine and orange juice into the dish, add the orange zest and boil hard for 5 mins. Add the meat and onions back in.

STEP 4

When ready to cook, heat oven to 160C/140C fan/gas 3. Stir the stock, canned tomatoes, potatoes and olives into the casserole, then bring to a simmer. Prod the potatoes as far under the surface of the liquid as you can. Cover, leaving a slight gap to one side, then cook in the oven for 2½ hrs, or until the meat is tender enough to cut with a spoon. Spoon away any excess fat and let the stew rest for a few mins before ladling into shallow bowls.

Squash, lentil & bean one-pot with fig raita

Prep:30 mins **Cook:**15 mins

Serves 2

Ingredients

- 400g piece butternut squash , peeled, deseeded and chunkily diced
- 1 onion , sliced
- 1 tbsp olive oil
- 2 tsp ground cumin
- ½ tsp chilli flakes
- 400g can chopped tomato
- 100g dried red lentil
- 2 tsp agave syrup or brown sugar
- 2 tsp red or white wine vinegar
- 400g can kidney bean , drained and rinsed
- 2 dried figs , finely chopped
- 150ml pot fat-free natural yogurt
- ½ small bunch parsley , chopped

Method

STEP 1

Fry the squash and onion in the oil for 5-8 mins until the onion is softened. Stir in the cumin and chilli for 1 min. Add the tomatoes plus a canful of water from the tomato can, the lentils, agave or sugar and vinegar. Bring to a simmer and cook for 10 mins, then stir in the beans and cook for a further few mins until the lentils are tender and the beans heated through.

STEP 2

Meanwhile, mix the figs, yogurt and parsley together. Season the stew, then serve in bowls with fig raita on the side.

One-pot beef brisket & braised celery

Prep:30 mins **Cook:**5 hrs

Serves 8

Ingredients

- 2.2kg piece of rolled beef brisket
- 1 bottle full-bodied red wine
- 3 tbsp olive oil
- 8 celery sticks , cut into little-finger-length pieces
- 2 carrots , roughly chopped
- 1 onion , sliced
- 3 garlic cloves , roughly chopped
- 4 thyme sprigs
- 4 bay leaves
- small pack parsley , roughly chopped

Method

STEP 1

If you have time, up to 24 hrs before, sit the beef in a snug plastic container and pour over the wine. Cover and leave to marinate in the fridge, turning the beef as and when you can.

STEP 2

Heat oven to 170C/150C fan/gas 3½. Drain the wine from the beef (if you've marinated), but keep the wine. Heat the oil in a flameproof casserole dish that will fit the beef and all the vegetables – don't worry if the beef is too tall for the dish. Season the beef and spend a good 15 mins browning it on all sides, then remove from the dish. Add the celery, carrots and onion to the dish, sizzle in the beef fat for 5 mins, then add the garlic and herbs. Nestle the beef among the vegetables, pour over the wine and bring to a simmer. Cover the dish with its lid (or foil if the beef is too tall) and braise in the oven for 4-4½ hrs until very tender, turning the beef once.

STEP 3

Once cooked, leave to rest for 10 mins, then lift the beef onto a carving board. Drain the vegetables (reserving the braising juices), toss with the parsley and tip into a dish. Spoon the fat off the braising juices and pour into a bowl for spooning over. *The sauce can be chilled in the fridge – the fat will solidify and can be lifted off the sauce before it's reheated.*

Speedy salmon and leek one-pot

Cook:25 mins

Serves 4

Ingredients

- 700g leeks , finely sliced
- 3 tbsp olive oil
- 2 tbsp wholegrain mustard
- 2 tbsp clear honey

- juice of half a lemon
- 250g pack cherry tomatoes , halved
- 4 skinless salmon fillets , about 175g/6oz each

Method

STEP 1

Cook the leeks: Put the leeks into a large microwave dish and sprinkle over 2 tablespoons water. Cover the dish with cling film and pierce a couple of times with a fork. Cook on 850W for 3 minutes, then leave to stand for 1 minute.

STEP 2

Make the sauce: Whisk the olive oil, mustard, honey and lemon juice together and season with a little salt and pepper. Scatter the tomatoes on top of the leeks and spoon over half the sauce.

STEP 3

Cook the salmon: Lay the salmon fillets side by side on top of the vegetables and spoon the remaining sauce over them. Replace the cling film and continue cooking on 850W for 9 minutes. Leave to stand for a couple of minutes before serving.

One-pot chicken with braised vegetables

Prep:20 mins **Cook:**1 hr and 30 mins

Serves 4

Ingredients

- 1 ½kg chicken
- 25g butter
- 200g smoked back bacon , preferably from a whole piece, cut into small chunks
- 1kg new potato , peeled

- 16-20 shallot or small onions
- ½ bottle white wine
- 250g pea , frozen are fine
- bunch soft green herbs such as tarragon , chives or parsley, chopped

Method

STEP 1

Heat oven to 220C/fan 200C/gas 7. Season the chicken inside and out with salt and pepper. Heat the butter in a casserole dish until sizzling, then take 10 mins to brown the chicken on all sides. Remove the chicken from the dish, then fry the bacon until crisp. Add the potatoes and shallots, then cook until just starting to brown. Nestle the chicken among the veg, pour over the wine, then pot-roast, undisturbed, for 1 hr or until the chicken is cooked.

STEP 2

After 1 hr, remove the chicken and place the pan back on the heat. Stir the peas into the buttery juices, adding a splash of water if the pan is dry, then simmer until the peas are cooked through. Finally, add any juices from the rested chicken, then stir through the herbs and serve with the chicken.

Sea bass & seafood Italian one-pot

Prep: 15 mins **Cook:** 45 mins

Serves 4

Ingredients

- 2 tbsp olive oil
- 1 fennel bulb , halved and sliced, fronds kept separate to garnish
- 2 garlic cloves , sliced
- ½ red chilli , chopped
- 250g cleaned squid , sliced into rings

- bunch basil , leaves and stalks separated, stalks tied together, leaves roughly chopped
- 400g can chopped tomato
- 150ml white wine
- 2 large handfuls of mussels or clams
- 8 large raw prawns (whole look nicest)
- 4 sea bass fillets (about 140g/5oz each)

- crusty bread , to serve

Method

STEP 1

Heat the oil in a large saucepan with a tight-fitting lid, then add the fennel, garlic and chilli. Fry until softened, then add the squid, basil stalks, tomatoes and wine. Simmer over a low heat for 35 mins until the squid is tender and the sauce has thickened slightly, then season.

STEP 2

Scatter the mussels and prawns over the sauce, lay the sea bass fillets on top, cover, turn up the heat and cook hard for 5 mins. Serve scattered with the basil leaves and fennel fronds, with crusty bread.

Bean & bangers one-pot

Prep: 10 mins **Cook:** 30 mins

Serves 4

Ingredients

- 1 tbsp olive oil
- 8 good-quality pork sausages (Toulouse or Sicilian varieties work well)
- 2 carrots , halved lengthways and sliced
- 2 onions , finely chopped
- 2 tbsp red wine vinegar
- 2 x 410g cans mixed beans in water, rinsed and drained
- 400ml chicken stock
- 100g frozen pea
- 2 tbsp Dijon mustard

Method

STEP 1

Heat the oil in a large pan. Sizzle the sausages for about 6 mins, turning occasionally, until brown on all sides, then remove to a plate. Tip the carrots and onions into the pan, then cook for 8 mins, stirring occasionally, until the onions are soft. Add the vinegar to the pan, then stir in the drained beans. Pour over the stock, nestle the sausages in with the beans, then simmer everything for 10 mins.

STEP 2

Scatter in the frozen peas, cook for 2 mins more until heated through, then take off the heat and stir in the mustard. Season to taste. Serve scooped straight from the pan.

One-pot chicken & chickpea pilau

Prep:10 mins **Cook:**30 mins

Serves 4

Ingredients

- 1 tbsp olive oil
- 4 chicken thighs , skin removed and trimmed of fat
- 2 large leeks , thinly sliced
- 2 garlic cloves , crushed
- 400g can chickpeas in water, drained and rinsed
- grated zest of 1 lemon
- 200g easy-cook brown rice
- 450ml chicken stock
- 1 head broccoli , broken into florets

Method

STEP 1

Heat a large, lidded frying pan or fl ameproof casserole and add the oil. Fry the chicken thighs for 2 mins, turning halfway through cooking, until lightly coloured, then lift onto a plate. Add the leeks to the pan and stir-fry for 3 mins, then add the garlic and tip in the chickpeas, most of the lemon zest and rice. Stir together until well mixed.

STEP 2

Nestle the chicken in the rice mix. Pour over the stock and season lightly. Cover and cook on a low heat for 20 mins until the chicken is nearly cooked through and the rice has absorbed nearly all the liquid. Sit the broccoli on top of the rice, cover and continue to cook until the rice and broccoli are tender and the chicken cooked. Sprinkle with the remaining lemon zest to serve.

One-pot cabbage & beans with white fish

Prep:20 mins **Cook:**30 mins

Serves 4

Ingredients

- small knob of butter
- 5 rashers smoked streaky bacon , chopped
- 1 onion , finely chopped
- 2 celery sticks, diced
- 2 carrots , diced

For the fish

- 4 fillets sustainable white fish , such as hake, about 140g/5oz each, skin on

- small bunch thyme
- 1 Savoy cabbage , shredded
- 4 tbsp white wine
- 300ml chicken stock
- 410g can flageolet bean in water, drained

- 2 tbsp plain flour
- 2 tbsp olive oil

Method

STEP 1

Heat the butter in a large sauté pan until starting to sizzle, add the bacon, then fry for a few mins. Add the onion, celery and carrots, then gently cook for 8-10 mins until softening, but not brown. Stir in the thyme and cabbage, then cook for a few mins until the cabbage starts to wilt. Pour in the wine, simmer until evaporated, then add the stock and beans. Season, cover the pan, then simmer gently for 10 mins until the cabbage is soft but still vibrant.

STEP 2

When the cabbage is done, cook the fish. Season each fillet, then dust the skin with flour. Heat the oil in a frying pan. Fry the fish, skin-side down, for 4 mins until crisp, then flip over and finish on the flesh side until cooked through. Serve each fish fillet on top of a pile of cabbage with a few small potatoes, if you like.

One-pot lentil chicken

Total time40 mins Ready in 40 minutes

Serves 2

Ingredients

- 1 tsp vegetable oil
- 2rasher lean dry-cure back bacon , trimmed and chopped
- 2large bone-in chicken thighs , skin removed
- 1medium onion , thinly sliced
- 1 garlic clove , thinly sliced

- 2 tsp plain flour
- 2 tsp tomato purée
- 150ml dry white wine
- 200ml chicken stock
- 50g green lentil
- ½ tsp dried thyme
- 85g chestnut mushroom , halved if large

Method

STEP 1

Heat the oil in a non-stick wide, shallow pan, add bacon and fry briskly until lightly coloured, then lift on to a plate. Add the chicken and fry on each side until lightly brown. Set aside with the bacon. Tip onion and garlic into the pan and cook for 5 minutes. Stir in the flour and tomato purée, then stir over a low heat for 2-3 minutes. Add the wine, stock, lentils and thyme. Bring to the boil, reduce the heat, cover and simmer for 5 minutes.

STEP 2

Stir in the mushrooms. Add the bacon and chicken, pushing them under the liquid. Cover and simmer for 20-25 minutes, or until lentils are tender and the chicken cooked. Season with salt and pepper.

Sausage & bean one-pot

Prep: 15 mins **Cook:** 30 mins

Serves 4

Ingredients

- 1 tbsp olive oil
- 8 good-quality pork sausages (Toulouse are great for this dish)
- 2 leeks , trimmed and thinly sliced
- 1 carrot , roughly chopped
- 2 slices day-old white or brown bread , whizzed into breadcrumbs

- 1 tbsp chopped sage , plus a little extra
- 1 garlic clove , crushed
- 200ml beef stock
- 400g can chopped tomatoes
- 2 x 400g cans cannellini beans , rinsed and drained

Method

STEP 1

Heat the oil in a large ovenproof pan, add the sausages and brown for few mins. Remove from the pan. Add the leeks and carrot and gently soften for 10 mins.

STEP 2

Mix the breadcrumbs with a little sage. Heat grill to medium. Add 1 tbsp sage and the garlic to the pan. Cook for 1 min, then add the stock and tomatoes. Tuck in the sausages. Simmer for 10 mins until the sauce has reduced a little and the sausages are cooked. Season, stir in the beans, then simmer for 2 mins more. To serve, scatter the sage crumbs over the top and grill for 5 mins until golden.

Pancakes for one

Prep: 10 mins **Cook:** 10 mins

Serves 1

Ingredients

- 1 large egg
- 40g plain flour
- ½ tsp baking powder
- 45ml milk (dairy, nut or oat based)

- 1 tsp butter
- ½ tbsp oil
- maple syrup or honey and berries, to serve (optional)

Method

STEP 1

Separate the egg, putting the white and yolk in seperate bowls. Mix the egg yolk with the flour, baking powder and milk to make a smooth paste.

STEP 2

Beat the egg white and a pinch of salt with an electric whisk (or by hand) until fluffy and holding its shape. Gently fold the egg white into the yolk mixture. Be extra careful not to knock any of the air out.

STEP 3

Heat the butter and oil in a non-stick frying pan. Dollop a third of the mixture into the pan and cook on each side for 1-2 mins or until golden brown. Repeat with the remaining mixture to make three pancakes. Drizzle over some maple syrup or honey and serve with berries, if you like.

Chinese pork one-pot

Total time15 mins

Serves 4

Ingredients

- 400g pork tenderloin , cut into long thin strips
- 600ml chicken stock
- 1 tbsp soy sauce
- 2 tsp Chinese five-spice powder
- large knob of ginger , peeled and cut into matchsticks
- 200g pack baby leaf green quartered
- 1 red chilli , deseeded and finely chopped or 1 tsp chilli flakes
- bunch spring onions , whites and greens sliced

Method

STEP 1

Tip all the ingredients, except the spring onion greens, into a large saucepan, put the lid on and bring to a gentle simmer. Cook, without boiling, for about 8 mins, until the pork has changed colour and the greens are cooked, but still a bit crunchy. Ladle into bowls, scatter with the spring onion and serve with boiled rice or noodles on the side.

One-pot roast pork chops with fennel & potatoes

Prep:10 mins **Cook:**50 mins

Serves 4

Ingredients

- 2 potatoes , cut into 8 wedges
- 1 fennel bulb , cut into 8 wedges
- 1 red pepper , halved, deseeded and cut into 8 wedges
- 4 thyme sprigs

- 4 garlic cloves , unpeeled
- 1 tbsp sundried tomato paste
- 300ml hot chicken stock
- 4 bone-in pork loin chops

Method

STEP 1

Heat oven to 200C/180C fan/gas 6. Put the potatoes, fennel, pepper, thyme and garlic in a large roasting tin. Mix together the tomato paste and stock, then pour into the pan. Tightly cover with foil and cook for 30 mins. Take out of the oven and increase the temperature to 220C/200C fan/gas 7.

STEP 2

Remove the foil and place the pork in the roasting tin, nestling in between the veg. Season well and return to the oven for 15-20 mins more or until golden brown and cooked through. Serve with the pan juices drizzled over.

Chicken, kale & mushroom pot pie

Prep:10 mins **Cook:**40 mins

Serves 4

Ingredients

- 1 tbsp olive oil
- 1 large onion, finely chopped

- 3 thyme sprigs, leaves picked
- 2 garlic cloves, crushed

- 350g chicken breasts, cut into small chunks
- 250g chestnut mushrooms, sliced
- 300ml chicken stock
- 100g crème fraîche
- 1 tbsp wholegrain mustard
- 100g kale
- 2 tsp cornflour, mixed with 1 tbsp cold water
- 375g pack puff pastry, rolled into a circle slightly bigger than your dish
- 1 egg yolk, to glaze

Method

STEP 1

Heat 1/2 tbsp oil over a gentle heat in a flameproof casserole dish. Add the onion and cook for 5 mins until softening. Scatter over the thyme and garlic, and stir for 1 min. Turn up the heat and add the chicken, frying until golden but not fully cooked. Add the mushrooms and the remaining oil. Heat oven to 200C/180 fan/gas 6.

STEP 2

Add the stock, crème fraîche, mustard and kale, and season well. Add the cornflour mixture and stir until thickened a little.

STEP 3

Remove from the heat and cover with the puff pastry lid, pressing into the sides of the casserole dish. Slice a cross in the centre and glaze with the egg. Bake for 30 mins until the pastry is puffed up and golden.

Meatball black bean chilli

Prep: 10 mins **Cook:** 30 mins

Serves 4

Ingredients

- 2 tbsp olive oil
- 12 beef meatballs
- 1 onion, finely sliced
- 2 mixed peppers, sliced
- ½ large bunch coriander, leaves and stalks chopped
- 2 large garlic cloves, crushed
- 1 tsp hot smoked paprika
- 2 tsp ground cumin
- 1 heaped tbsp light brown soft sugar
- 2 x 400g cans chopped tomatoes

- 2 x 400g cans black beans, drained and   rinsed
- cooked rice, to serve

Method

STEP 1

Heat the oil in a large flameproof casserole dish over a medium heat. Fry the meatballs for 5 mins until browned, then transfer to a plate with a slotted spoon.

STEP 2

Fry the onion and peppers with a pinch of salt for 7 mins. Add the coriander stalks, garlic, paprika and cumin and fry for 1 min more. Tip in the sugar, tomatoes and beans, and bring to a simmer. Season, return the meatballs to the pan and cook, covered, for 15 mins. *To freeze, leave to cool completely and transfer to large freezerproof bags.*

STEP 3

Serve the chilli with the rice and the coriander leaves scattered over.

Spring chicken pot pie

Prep:15 mins **Cook:**1 hr and 5 mins

Serves 6

Ingredients

- 4-6 skinless, boneless chicken thighs
- 1 tbsp olive oil
- 100g smoked bacon lardons
- 2 leeks , sliced
- 3 tbsp plain flour
- 100ml white wine (or extra stock)
- 200ml chicken stock
- 200g crème fraîche
- 100g frozen or fresh podded peas
- 1½ tbsp Dijon mustard
- small bunch of tarragon , chopped
- 1 egg , beaten
- 320g sheet puff pastry

Method

STEP 1

Season the chicken thighs with some salt and pepper. Heat the oil in a heavy-based saucepan and fry the chicken for 3-4 mins on each side until lightly golden, then transfer to a plate. Add the bacon to the pan and fry for 5 mins until golden. Tip in the leeks and fry for another 5 mins.

STEP 2

Sprinkle the flour over the leeks and bacon, and stir until combined. Add the wine, if using, and bubble for a few minutes, then add the stock and stir well. Slice the chicken and return it to the pan – don't worry if it's not fully cooked through at this point, it will finish cooking in the oven.

STEP 3

Stir in the crème fraîche, peas, 1 tbsp mustard and the tarragon, and bubble for a few minutes until thick and saucy. Add a splash more stock or water if it seems too thick Remove the pie filling from the heat. Whisk the remaining ½ tbsp mustard with the egg in a bowl.

STEP 4

Heat the oven to 200C/180C fan/gas 6. Spoon the filling into a pie dish with a lip and use some of the egg mix to brush the sides of the dish. Unroll the pastry over the top of the pie and crimp the edges against the sides of the dish, then cut away any excess with a knife. *Will keep frozen, well covered, for up to three months.*

STEP 5

Brush the remaining egg glaze over the pie and make a small steam hole in the middle. Bake for 40 mins until golden and puffed. Serve with buttered new potatoes and steamed greens or carrots, if you like.

One-pot roast guinea fowl

Prep: 20 mins **Cook:** 1 hr and 40 mins

Serves 2

Ingredients

- 1 onion , cut into wedges, through the root
- 2 carrots , quartered lengthways
- 1 large potato , cut into bite-size chunks
- 1 tbsp olive oil
- 1 small guinea fowl (around 1kg/2lb 4oz)

- 1 tbsp butter at room temperature, plus 2 tsp for the gravy
- 4 smoked streaky bacon rashers
- 6 garlic cloves , unpeeled
- few thyme sprigs
- 300ml chicken stock
- 100ml white wine
- 2 tsp plain flour
- 1 tbsp redcurrant jelly

Method

STEP 1

Heat oven to 180C/160C fan/gas 4. Toss the vegetables with the oil and some seasoning in a large flameproof roasting tin. Place the bird on top of the veg, smear with 1 tbsp butter and lay the rashers in a row over the breast. Season generously, then roast for 40 mins.

STEP 2

Remove from the oven and give the veg a stir while adding the garlic and thyme. Pour 200ml stock and the wine over the veg and return to oven to roast for another 40 mins until the bird is cooked through and the juices run clear.

STEP 3

Remove the bird, place on a serving plate, cover with foil to keep warm and leave to rest. Turn the oven up to 200C/180C fan/gas 6 and roast the veg for a further 15 mins until tender.

STEP 4

Remove the veg with a slotted spoon and transfer to the serving plate with the bird. Mix 2 tsp butter and flour in a small bowl to form a smooth paste. Place the roasting tin with all the cooking juices, plus any resting juices, on the hob. Whisk the paste and redcurrant jelly into the juices until dissolved, then add the remaining stock and extra seasoning, if you like. Bubble for a few mins until the sauce thickens. Slice and serve the guinea fowl, crisp bacon and the veg with the sauce on the side.

Creamy chicken stew

Prep:10 mins **Cook:**55 mins

Serves 4-6

Ingredients

- 3 leeks , halved and finely sliced
- 2 tbsp olive oil , plus extra if needed
- 1 tbsp butter
- 8 small chicken thighs
- 500ml chicken stock
- 1 tbsp Dijon mustard
- 75g crème fraîche
- 200g frozen peas
- 3 tbsp dried or fresh breadcrumbs
- small bunch of parsley , finely chopped

Method

STEP 1

Tip the leeks and oil into a flameproof casserole dish on a low heat, add the butter and cook everything very gently for 10 mins or until the leeks are soft.

STEP 2

Put the chicken, skin-side down, in a large non-stick frying pan on a medium heat, cook until the skin browns, then turn and brown the other side. You shouldn't need any oil but if the skin starts to stick, add a little. Add the chicken to the leeks, leaving behind any fat in the pan.

STEP 3

Add the stock to the dish and bring to a simmer, season well, cover and cook for 30 mins on low. Stir in the mustard, crème fraîche and peas and bring to a simmer. You should have quite a bit of sauce.

STEP 4

When you're ready to serve, put the grill on. Mix the breadcrumbs and parsley, sprinkle them over the chicken and grill until browned.

Spinach, sweet potato & lentil dhal

Prep:10 mins **Cook:**35 mins

Serves 4

Ingredients

- 1 tbsp sesame oil
- 1 red onion, finely chopped
- 1 garlic clove, crushed
- thumb-sized piece ginger, peeled and finely chopped
- 1 red chilli, finely chopped
- 1 ½ tsp ground turmeric

- 1 ½ tsp ground cumin
- 2 sweet potatoes (about 400g/14oz), cut into even chunks
- 250g red split lentils
- 600ml vegetable stock
- 80g bag of spinach
- 4 spring onions, sliced on the diagonal, to serve
- ½ small pack of Thai basil, leaves torn, to serve

Method

STEP 1

Heat 1 tbsp sesame oil in a wide-based pan with a tight-fitting lid.

STEP 2

Add 1 finely chopped red onion and cook over a low heat for 10 mins, stirring occasionally, until softened.

STEP 3

Add 1 crushed garlic clove, a finely chopped thumb-sized piece of ginger and 1 finely chopped red chilli, cook for 1 min, then add 1 ½ tsp ground turmeric and 1 ½ tsp ground cumin and cook for 1 min more.

STEP 4

Turn up the heat to medium, add 2 sweet potatoes, cut into even chunks, and stir everything together so the potato is coated in the spice mixture.

STEP 5

Tip in 250g red split lentils, 600ml vegetable stock and some seasoning.

STEP 6

Bring the liquid to the boil, then reduce the heat, cover and cook for 20 mins until the lentils are tender and the potato is just holding its shape.

STEP 7

Taste and adjust the seasoning, then gently stir in the 80g spinach. Once wilted, top with the 4 diagonally sliced spring onions and ½ small pack torn basil leaves to serve.

STEP 8

Alternatively, allow to cool completely, then divide between airtight containers and store in the fridge for a healthy lunchbox.

Peach & orange yogurt pots with ginger oats

Prep:10 mins **Cook:**7 mins

Makes 4

Ingredients

- 4 peaches or nectarines, stoned and diced
- 1 orange , juiced and zested
- 120g porridge oats
- 25g pine nuts

- ½ tsp ground ginger
- 1 tsp ground cinnamon
- 2 tbsp sultanas
- 4 x 150ml pots bio yogurt

Method

STEP 1

Put the peaches and orange juice in a small pan. Put the lid on and cook gently for 3-5 mins, depending on their ripeness, until softened. Set aside to cool.

STEP 2

Tip the oats and pine nuts into a pan and heat gently, stirring frequently until they're just starting to toast. Turn off the heat and add the spices, zest and sultanas.

STEP 3

Spoon the peaches and juices into four tumblers and top with the yogurt. Cover and chill until needed. Keep the oat mixture in an airtight container. When ready to serve, top the peaches and yogurt with the oat mixture.

Curried cod

Prep:10 mins **Cook:**25 mins

Serves 4

Ingredients

- 1 tbsp oil
- 1 onion, chopped
- 2 tbsp medium curry powder
- thumb-sized piece ginger, peeled and finely grated
- 3 garlic cloves, crushed

- 2 x 400g cans chopped tomatoes
- 400g can chickpeas
- 4 cod fillets (about 125-150g each)
- zest 1 lemon, then cut into wedges
- handful coriander, roughly chopped

Method

STEP 1

Heat the oil in a large, lidded frying pan. Cook the onion over a high heat for a few mins, then stir in the curry powder, ginger and garlic. Cook for another 1-2 mins until fragrant, then stir in the tomatoes, chickpeas and some seasoning.

STEP 2

Cook for 8-10 mins until thickened slightly, then top with the cod. Cover and cook for another 5-10 mins until the fish is cooked through. Scatter over the lemon zest and coriander, then serve with the lemon wedges to squeeze over.

Pot-roast Bombay chicken

Prep:20 mins **Cook:**1 hr and 30 mins

Serves 4 - 6

Ingredients

- 1 small whole chicken
- 5 tbsp tikka masala paste
- 1 tbsp sunflower oil
- 1 large red onion, halved and sliced
- 2 large tomatoes, halved and chopped
- 1 tbsp fenugreek seeds
- 1 thumb-sized piece ginger, grated

- 2 x 400g cans full-fat coconut milk
- 500g new potatoes, halved
- 100g baby spinach
- 25g pack coriander, torn, to serve
- poppadums and chutney, to serve (optional)

Method

STEP 1

Heat oven to 220C/200C fan/gas 6. Put the chicken on a chopping board and, using your hands, rub the skin generously with half the spice paste. Season well, tie the legs together and set aside.

STEP 2

Heat the oil in a large flameproof casserole dish over a medium heat. Add the onion and a good pinch of salt and cook for 5 mins or until beginning to soften. Add the tomatoes, fenugreek seeds, ginger and remaining spice paste, and cook for 3 mins more. Stir through the coconut milk and bring to a simmer. Add the chicken and the potatoes to the dish, and cook in the oven for 20 mins, uncovered.

STEP 3

Lower the heat to 180C/160C fan/ gas 4 and cook for 55 mins more. Check that the meat is cooked by cutting through one of its legs – the flesh shouldn't be pink.

STEP 4

Remove the chicken and place on a chopping board. Stir the spinach through the sauce and leave to rest for 5 mins. Put the chicken back in the dish, top with the coriander and carve at the table. Serve with poppadums and chutney, if you like.

One-pan Thai green salmon

Prep: 10 mins **Cook:** 50 mins

Serves 4

Ingredients

- 2 tbsp vegetable oil
- 2 shallots , thickly sliced
- 1 green chilli , deseeded if you like, and sliced, plus extra to serve
- 300g baby new potatoes , quartered
- 1 lemongrass stalk, bashed
- 4 tbsp Thai green curry paste
- 400g can coconut milk
- 200-300ml vegetable stock
- 1-2 tbsp fish sauce
- ½-1 tbsp brown or palm sugar
- 1 courgette , trimmed and peeled into ribbons
- 100g baby spinach
- 4 skinless salmon fillets
- 3 limes , 2 juiced plus 1 cut into wedges to serve
- 3 spring onions , finely sliced (optional)
- handful of coriander or Thai basil, roughly chopped, to serve

- cooked jasmine rice or rice noodles, to serve (optional)

Method

STEP 1

Heat the oven to 200C/180C fan/ gas 6. Put the oil in a deep roasting tin or dish about 30 x 25cm and toss through the shallots, chilli, potatoes and lemongrass. Roast for 10 mins until fragrant, keeping an eye on the shallots to ensure they don't burn. Remove from the oven and stir in the curry paste to coat everything. Return to the oven for 2 mins until its aroma is released before mixing in the coconut milk and 200ml stock. Put back in the oven again for 15-20 mins until the sauce is slightly thickened and the potatoes are turning tender.

STEP 2

Season to taste with the fish sauce and sugar, then stir through the courgette ribbons and spinach. Add another 50ml-100ml stock now if the sauce is too thick, but be aware that the courgette and spinach will release some water as well. Nestle the salmon fillets in the sauce and bake for a further 10-15 mins until the salmon is cooked to your liking.

STEP 3

Add the lime juice and taste the sauce for a balance of sweet and sour, adding more lime juice and fish sauce, if you like. Scatter over the spring onions, if using, along with the herbs and chilli. For a more filling meal, serve with rice or noodles and the lime wedges on the side.

Herby spring chicken pot pie

Prep: 10 mins **Cook:** 30 mins

Serves 4

Ingredients

- 2 tbsp olive oil , plus a little extra for brushing over the pastry
- bunch spring onions , sliced into 3cm pieces
- 250g frozen spinach
- 6 ready-cooked chicken thighs (or see tip, below)
- 350ml hot chicken stock
- ½ tbsp wholegrain mustard
- 200g frozen peas
- 200ml half-fat crème fraîche
- ½ small bunch tarragon , leaves finely chopped
- small bunch parsley , finely chopped

- 270g pack filo pastry

Method

STEP 1

Heat oven to 200C/180C fan/gas 6. Heat the oil in a large, shallow casserole dish on a medium heat. Add the spring onions and fry for 3 mins, then stir through the frozen spinach and cook for 2 mins or until it's starting to wilt. Remove the skin from the chicken and discard. Shred the chicken off the bone and into the pan, and discard the bones. Stir through the stock and mustard. Bring to a simmer and cook, uncovered, for 5-10 mins.

STEP 2

Stir in the peas, crème fraîche and herbs, then remove from the heat. Scrunch the filo pastry sheets over the mixture, brush with a little oil and bake for 15-20 mins or until golden brown.

One-pot fish with black olives & tomatoes

Prep:10 mins **Cook:**15 mins - 20 mins

Serves 4

Ingredients

- 175g black olive in oil, stones removed
- 1large onion , roughly chopped
- 400g can chopped tomato

To serve

- chopped parsley

- 4 boneless white fish fillets such as Icelandic cod or hoki, each weighing about 175g/6oz

- lemon wedges

Method

STEP 1

Preheat the oven to fan 180C/conventional 200C/gas 6. Heat 1 tbsp of the oil from the olives in an ovenproof pan. Tip in the onion and stir well, leave to cook for a minute or two and then give it another good stir. Add the tomatoes and some salt and pepper. Bring to the boil, then add the olives.

STEP 2

Put the fish, skin side down, onto the sauce and drizzle over a splash more oil from the olive jar. Bake, uncovered, for 15 minutes until the fish is cooked. Sprinkle with chopped parsley and serve straight from the pan, with lemon wedges for squeezing over.

Baked tomato & mozzarella orzo

Prep:10 mins **Cook:**30 mins

Serves 2

Ingredients

- 150g orzo
- ½ tbsp olive oil
- 2 roasted red peppers from a jar, roughly chopped
- handful olives , roughly chopped
- big pinch chilli flakes

- ½ tsp dried oregano
- 400g can chopped tomatoes with garlic (if you can't find ready mixed, crush 1 garlic clove into a can of tomatoes)
- 125g ball mozzarella

Method

STEP 1

Heat oven to 200C/180C fan/gas 6. Tip the orzo into a medium casserole dish, then stir in the oil, red peppers, olives, chilli flakes and dried oregano. Tip in the chopped tomatoes, then refill the can halfway with water and pour that in too. Give everything a good mix, season, then cover and bake for 20 mins until the pasta is almost cooked. Take it out of the oven and give the orzo a stir. Remove the foil and return to the oven for a further 5 mins.

STEP 2

Heat the grill to high. Take the orzo out of the oven and tear the mozzarella over the top, then grill until melted and bubbling. Serve with salad on the side, if you like.

Quick beef & broccoli one-pot

Prep:10 mins **Cook:**10 mins

Serves 4

Ingredients

- 1 tbsp olive oil
- 50g unsalted cashew nuts
- 400g frying beef steak, cut into strips
- 1 large head broccoli , broken into florets
- 4 sticks celery , sliced
- 150ml beef stock (from a cube is fine)
- 2 tbsp horseradish sauce
- 2 tbsp low-fat fromage frais

Method

STEP 1

Heat the oil in a frying pan, add the nuts and toss for a few secs until lightly toasted. Set aside.

STEP 2

Season the steak strips with plenty of pepper and stir-fry over a high heat for 1-2 mins to brown. Set aside with the nuts. Tip the broccoli and celery into the pan and stir-fry for 2 mins. Pour the stock over, cover and simmer for 2 mins. Meanwhile, mix the horseradish and fromage frais together.

STEP 3

Return the steak to the pan and toss with the veg, then sprinkle over the nuts and serve with the creamy horseradish. Great with mashed potatoes.

Spicy vegetable & quinoa one-pot

Prep:5 mins **Cook:**15 mins

Serves 4

Ingredients

- 1 onion , sliced
- 4 tbsp vegetarian korma or Madras curry paste
- 1l milk
- 750g frozen mixed vegetable
- 175g quinoa , rinsed

Method

STEP 1

Simmer the onion and the curry paste with a splash of water for 5 mins in a large saucepan, stirring from time to time. Heat the milk in a jug in the microwave.

STEP 2

Add the vegetables and quinoa, then stir in the milk. Bring to the boil, simmer gently for 10 mins until the quinoa is cooked. Check seasoning. Serve with warm naan bread.

Honey & mustard chicken thighs with spring veg

Prep:10 mins **Cook:**40 mins

Serves 2

Ingredients

- 1 tbsp honey
- 1 tbsp wholegrain mustard
- 2 garlic cloves, crushed
- zest and juice 1 lemon
- 4 chicken thighs, skin on

- 300g new potatoes, unpeeled, smaller left whole, bigger halved
- 1 tbsp olive oil
- 100g spinach
- 100g frozen peas

Method

STEP 1

Heat oven to 200C/180C fan/gas 6. In a small bowl, mix together the honey, mustard, garlic and the lemon zest and juice. Pour the marinade over the chicken thighs and season.

STEP 2

Put the chicken, skin-side up, on a large baking tray, then dot the new potatoes in between them. Drizzle the oil over the potatoes and sprinkle with sea salt. Roast in the oven for 35 mins until the chicken skin caramelises and is charred in places.

STEP 3

Add the spinach and peas to the roasting tray. Return to the oven for 2-3 mins until the spinach has begun to wilt and the peas are hot and covered in the mustardy sauce.

Spiced coconut chicken with coriander & lime

Prep:20 mins **Cook:**1 hr

Serves 4-6

Ingredients

- 1 tbsp oil
- 8 skin-on and bone-in chicken thighs
- 1 large onion , roughly chopped
- 4 garlic cloves , grated to a purée
- 3cm piece ginger , peeled and grated
- ½ tsp turmeric
- 2 tsp ground cumin
- 2 green chillies , halved, deseeded and finely chopped
- 200g butternut squash , peeled, deseeded and cut into slices (prepared weight)
- 100g cauliflower florets
- 225g basmati rice
- 10g bunch coriander , chopped
- 2 limes , zested and juiced
- 2 lime leaves
- 300ml coconut milk
- 400ml chicken stock

Method

STEP 1

Heat oven to 200C/180C fan/gas 6. Heat the oil in a 30cm shallow casserole dish or high-sided frying pan. Fry the chicken thighs, skin-side down, just to get some colour on them (they will take on a deeper colour in the oven). Transfer them to another dish. Fry the onion in the pan until soft and pale gold. Add the garlic, spices and chillies. Cook for 2 mins more, then stir in the squash, cauliflower, rice, half the coriander, the lime zest, half the lime juice, the lime leaves and some seasoning. Put the chicken back in the pan, this time skin-side up, and season that as well.

STEP 2

Heat the coconut milk and the chicken stock together until just below boiling point. Pour this around the chicken and put the pan in the oven, uncovered. Cook for 40 mins, or until the chicken is cooked through and the liquid has been absorbed by the rice. Squeeze over the remaining lime and scatter with the rest of the coriander. You could gently push the coriander into the rice, so it's not all on top. Serve immediately.

Curried mango & chickpea pot

Prep: 15 mins

Serves 1

Ingredients

- 200g chickpeas , drained and rinsed
- 2 tbsp fat-free Greek yogurt
- ½ lemon , juiced
- 1 heaped tbsp korma curry paste
- ½ carrot , julienned or grated
- 70g red cabbage , shredded
- 50g baby spinach , shredded
- 40g mango , finely diced
- ½ tsp nigella seeds
- ½ small red chilli , finely sliced (deseeded if you want less heat)

Method

STEP 1

Combine the chickpeas, yogurt, lemon and korma paste in a bowl, then toss with the carrot, cabbage, spinach and mango. Tip into your lunchbox or an airtight container and scatter with the nigella seeds and red chilli.

Slow-cooker chicken curry

Prep: 10 mins **Cook:** 6 hrs

Serves 2

Ingredients

- 1 large onion, roughly chopped
- 3 tbsp mild curry paste
- 400g can chopped tomatoes
- 2 tsp vegetable bouillon powder
- 1 tbsp finely chopped ginger
- 1 yellow pepper, deseeded and chopped
- 2 skinless chicken legs, fat removed
- 30g pack fresh coriander, leaves chopped
- cooked brown rice, to serve

Method

STEP 1

Put 1 roughly chopped large onion, 3 tbsp mild curry paste, a 400g can chopped tomatoes, 2 tsp vegetable bouillon powder, 1 tbsp finely chopped ginger and 1 chopped yellow pepper into the slow cooker pot with a third of a can of water and stir well.

STEP 2

Add 2 skinless chicken legs, fat removed, and push them under all the other ingredients so that they are completely submerged. Cover with the lid and chill in the fridge overnight.

STEP 3

The next day, cook on Low for 6 hrs until the chicken and vegetables are really tender.

STEP 4

Stir in the the chopped leaves of 30g coriander just before serving over brown rice.

Vegetarian bean pot with herby breadcrumbs

Prep:10 mins **Cook:**35 mins

Serves 2

Ingredients

- 1 slice crusty bread
- ½ small pack parsley leaves
- ½ lemon , zested
- 2 tbsp olive oil
- pinch chilli flakes (optional)
- 2 leeks , rinsed and chopped into half-moons
- 2 carrots , thinly sliced

- 2 celery sticks , thinly sliced
- 1 fennel bulb , thinly sliced
- 2 large garlic cloves , chopped
- 1 tbsp tomato purée
- few thyme sprigs
- 150ml white wine
- 400g can cannellini beans , drained

Method

STEP 1

Toast the bread, then tear into pieces and put in a food processor with the parsley, lemon zest, ½ tbsp olive oil, a good pinch of salt and pepper and the chilli flakes, if using. Blitz to breadcrumbs. Set aside.

STEP 2

Heat the remaining oil in a pan and add the leeks, carrots, celery and fennel along with a splash of water and a pinch of salt. Cook over a medium heat for 10 mins until soft, then add the garlic and tomato purée. Cook for 1 min more, then add the thyme and white wine. Leave to bubble for a minute, then add the beans. Fill the can halfway with water and pour into the pot.

STEP 3

Bring the cassoulet to the boil, then turn down the heat and leave to simmer for 15 mins before removing the thyme sprigs. Mash half the beans to thicken the stew. Season to taste, then divide between bowls and top with the herby breadcrumbs to serve.

Roast chicken traybake

Prep: 10 mins **Cook:** 1 hr and 5 mins

Serves 2

Ingredients

- 2 red onions (320g), sliced across into rings
- 1 large red pepper , deseeded and chopped into 3cm pieces
- 300g potatoes , peeled and cut into 3cm chunks
- 2 tbsp rapeseed oil
- 4 bone-in chicken thighs , skin and any fat removed

- 1 lime , zested and juiced
- 3 large garlic cloves , finely grated
- 1 tsp smoked paprika
- 1 tsp thyme leaves
- 2 tsp vegetable bouillon powder
- 200g long stem broccoli , stem cut into lengths if very thick

Method

STEP 1

Heat the oven to 200C/180C fan/gas 6. Put the onion, pepper, potatoes and oil in a non-stick roasting tin and toss everything together. Roast for 15 mins while you rub the chicken with the lime zest, garlic, paprika and thyme. Take the veg from the oven, stir, then snuggle the chicken thighs among the veg, covering them with some of the onions so they don't dry out as it roasts for 40 mins.

STEP 2

As you approach the end of the cooking time, mix 200ml boiling water with the bouillon powder. Take the roasting tin from the oven, add the broccoli to the tin, and pour over the hot stock followed by the lime juice, then quickly cover with the foil and put back in the oven for 10 more mins until the broccoli is just tender.

Courgette & lemon risotto

Prep: 10 mins **Cook:** 40 mins

Serves 2

Ingredients

- 50g butter
- 1 onion, finely chopped
- 1 large garlic clove, crushed
- 180g risotto rice
- 1 vegetable stock cube
- zest and juice 1 lemon

- 2 lemon thyme sprigs
- 250g courgette, diced
- 50g parmesan (or vegetarian alternative), grated
- 2 tbsp crème fraîche

Method

STEP 1

Melt the butter in a deep frying pan. Add the onion and fry gently until softened for about 8 mins, then add the garlic and stir for 1 min. Stir in the rice to coat it in the buttery onions and garlic for 1-2 mins.

STEP 2

Dissolve the stock cube in 1 litre of boiling water, then add a ladle of the stock to the rice, along with the lemon juice and thyme. Bubble over a medium heat, stirring constantly. When almost all the liquid has been absorbed, add another ladle of stock and keep stirring. Tip in the courgette and keep adding the stock, stirring every now and then until the rice is just tender and creamy.

STEP 3

To serve, stir in some seasoning, the lemon zest, Parmesan and crème fraîche.

Pot-roast chicken with stock

Prep:10 mins **Cook:**2 hrs and 10 mins

Serves 4 with leftovers

Ingredients

- 2 tbsp olive oil
- 2.4kg chicken – buy the best you can afford
- 4 onions , peeled and cut into large wedges

- ½ bunch thyme
- 3 garlic cloves
- 6 peppercorns
- 175ml white wine
- 1.2l chicken stock

Method

STEP 1

Heat oven to 170C/150C fan/gas 5. Heat the oil in a large flameproof casserole dish and brown the chicken well on all sides, then sit it breast-side up. Pack in the onions, thyme, garlic and peppercorns, pour over the wine and stock, and bring to the boil. Pop on the lid and transfer to the oven for 2 hrs.

STEP 2

Remove and rest for 20 mins. Carefully lift the chicken onto a chopping board and carve as much as you need. Serve the carved chicken in a shallow bowl with the onions and some of the stock poured over. Serve with some usual Sunday veg and roast potatoes.

STEP 3

Strain the leftover stock into a bowl and strip the carcass of all the chicken. Chill both for up to three days or freeze for up to a month to use for other recipes like our one-pot chicken noodle soup.

Vegan jambalaya

Prep:10 mins **Cook:**35 mins

Serves 2

Ingredients

- 2 tbsp cold-pressed rapeseed oil
- 1 large onion (180g), finely chopped
- 4 celery sticks , finely chopped
- 1 yellow pepper , chopped
- 2 tsp smoked paprika
- ½ tsp chilli flakes
- ½ tsp dried oregano

- 115g brown basmati rice
- 400g can chopped tomatoes
- 2 garlic cloves , finely grated
- 400g butter beans , drained and rinsed
- 2 tsp vegetable bouillon powder
- large handful of parsley , chopped

Method

STEP 1

Heat the oil in a large pan set over a high heat and fry the onion, celery and pepper, stirring occasionally, for 5 mins until starting to soften and colour.

STEP 2

Stir in the spices and rice, then tip in the tomatoes and a can of water. Stir in the garlic, beans and bouillon. Bring to a simmer, then cover and cook for 25 mins until the rice is tender and has absorbed most of the liquid. Keep an eye on the pan towards the end of the cooking time to make sure it doesn't boil dry – if it starts to catch, add a little more water. Stir in the parsley and serve hot.

Chicken tagine with lemons, olives & pomegranate

Prep:10 mins **Cook:**1 hr and 30 mins

Serves 4-5

Ingredients

- 2 tbsp olive oil
- 8 chicken thighs
- 1 onion , chopped
- 2 garlic cloves
- 2 tbsp Moroccan spice mix (see below)
- 1 large or 2 small preserved lemons , skin only, finely chopped

- 2 large tomatoes , chopped
- 1 chicken stock cube
- 1 tbsp honey
- 1 tbsp red wine vinegar
- handful olives
- 1 small lemon , 1/2 very thinly sliced
- ½ pomegranate , seeds only

- 100g feta , crumbled
- couscous , to serve
- small bunch mint , leaves only

For the Moroccan spice mix

- 2 tbsp coriander seeds
- 1 tbsp cumin seeds
- 1½ tsp fennel seeds
- ½ tsp black pepper
- ¼ tsp ground ginger
- 1 tsp ground cinnamon
- good pinch saffron

Method

STEP 1

Heat 1 tbsp oil in a wide, shallow casserole dish or ovenproof pan. Season the chicken and cook, skin-side down, for 8-10 mins, until crispy. Flip over and cook for another 5 mins. Transfer to a plate. Heat oven to 170C/150C fan/gas 3.

STEP 2

Add the rest of the oil and the onion to the pan. Stir for a few mins, then add the garlic and Moroccan spice mix. Stir, scraping any bits of onions and chicken from the bottom, until the spices smell fragrant. Add the preserved lemon, tomatoes, stock cube, honey, vinegar and 750ml water. Bring to the boil, then place the chicken on top. Cover with a lid or foil and transfer to the oven for 1 hr.

STEP 3

Uncover, place the olives and lemon slices on top and drizzle the lemons with a little oil. Return to the oven for 20 mins, or until the sauce has reduced a little (you can do this on the hob if you're short on time). Check the seasoning, adding a squeeze of lemon, more honey or salt if you think it needs it. Scatter over the pomegranate seeds, feta and mint, and serve with couscous.

Smoky bacon pot noodle for one

Prep: 2 mins **Cook:** 5 mins

Serves 1

Ingredients

- 1 rasher smoked back bacon , trimmed and chopped
- 2 spring onions , white and green separated and finely sliced
- 50g frozen pea
- quarter tsp paprika

- 2 tsp cornflour
- 200ml vegetable stock
- 150g block straight-to-wok wheat noodle , or equivalent of dried, cooked
- splash Worcestershire sauce

Method

STEP 1

In a small non-stick pan, fry the bacon for a few mins, add the white parts of the spring onions, peas and paprika, then cook for 1 min more. Mix the cornflour with a little of the stock to get a paste, then stir this into the pan with the rest of the stock, noodles and a good splash of Worcestershire sauce. Simmer for a couple of mins until thick and saucy, then scatter with the green parts of spring onion.

Potted cheddar with ale & mustard

Prep: 10 mins **Cook:** 5 mins

6-8 (1 x 400ml jar)

Ingredients

- 250g extra mature cheddar cheese , chopped
- 140g butter

- 1 tbsp ale
- 1 tbsp wholegrain mustard
- 1 thyme sprig (optional)

Method

STEP 1

Put the cheese, 100g butter and ale in a food processor. Blitz until creamy and well combined. Stir in the mustard, then pack into a large sterilised jar, ramekin or ceramic pot, making sure to eliminate any air pockets.

STEP 2

Melt the remaining butter and leave to sit for a minute to let the fat separate from the milk solids (these will form a milky puddle at the bottom). Pour the clear fat over the cheese, leaving the milk solids in the pan. Place a thyme sprig on top, if using, and chill for a few hours. The sealed cheese will keep for a couple of months in the fridge. Once you've cracked the buttery crust, use up within a week.

Peanut butter & date oat pots

Prep: 10 mins

Serves 6

Ingredients

- 180g porridge oats
- 75g 100% crunchy peanut butter
- 40g stoned medjool dates , chopped
- 2 tsp vanilla extract

- 5 x 120g pots plain bio yogurt (or 600g from a large pot)
- ground cinnamon , for dusting

Method

STEP 1

Tip the oats into a large bowl and pour over 600ml boiling water. Add the peanut butter, dates and vanilla and stir well. Cool, then stir through 240g of the yogurt. Dilute with a small amount of water if the consistency is a little stiff.

STEP 2

Spoon into six glasses, then top with the remaining yogurt and dust with cinnamon. Cover each glass and keep in the fridge until ready to eat. Will keep well for up to five days.

One-pan lamb with hasselback potatoes

Prep:30 mins **Cook:**2 hrs

Serves 6-8

Ingredients

- 1 leg of lamb , about 2kg
- 2 garlic bulbs
- 15 sprigs rosemary
- 15 sprigs thyme

- 1.7kg medium-sized potatoes (Maris Piper work well), unpeeled
- 14 bay leaves
- 4 tbsp olive oil
- 1 lemon , juiced

Method

STEP 1

Use a small, sharp knife to make at least 30 small, deep, incisions all over the lamb. Halve the garlic bulbs, so at the top the cloves fall away and at the bottom, they remain attached. Peel and slice the tops that have fallen away and keep the other halves for later. Use your fingers to push the slices into each slit. Next, pull off small sprigs of rosemary and thyme, keeping the stalks on, and poke them into the slits, too. Can be done a day ahead, then cover the lamb and chill. Remove from the fridge 1 hr before roasting.

STEP 2

Heat oven to 210C/190C fan/gas 7. Sit each potato between the handles of two wooden spoons and cut widthways at 3mm intervals – the spoon handles will stop you slicing all the way through. Slot a bay leaf into the middle slit of each potato. Tip the potatoes into a large roasting tin with the halved garlic bulb and the rest of the rosemary and thyme. Drizzle with half the oil and season, then toss to coat and turn the potatoes so they're all cut-side up. Nestle the lamb in the middle of the tin, pushing the potatoes to the outside, then rub the lamb with the rest of the oil and the lemon juice and season generously.

STEP 3

Roast for 1 hr 30 mins, basting the potatoes and shaking the tin occasionally, until the lamb is dark brown and the potatoes are crisp and golden. The lamb will be pink in the middle but cooked. For rare, cook for 10 mins less, and for well done, 15 mins more. Remove the lamb from the tin and leave to rest for 15 mins, putting the potatoes back in the oven if you need to. Serve drizzled with our green olive & herb dressing.

One-pan seafood roast with smoky garlic butter

Prep:20 mins **Cook:**40 mins

Serves 4

Ingredients

- 400g baby new potatoes
- 1 tbsp olive or rapeseed oil
- 2 corn cobs
- 8-12 large prawns , heads and shells on
- 8-12 mussels or large clams (or a mixture)
- 2 medium squids with tentacles, cleaned

- 150g butter
- small bunch parsley , chopped, plus a little to serve
- 1 tsp smoked paprika
- 3 garlic cloves , crushed
- 1 lemon , zested then cut into wedges
- 200g ring chorizo , peeled and sliced

Method

STEP 1

Heat oven to 200C/180C fan/gas 6. Use a large knife to hasselback the potatoes; cut incisions in each potato making sure you don't cut through to the base, and keep the cuts as close together as possible. Toss the potatoes in oil and some seasoning in your largest roasting tin (an oven tray is ideal – line with parchment first if it's old). Roast for 20 mins.

STEP 2

Butterfly the prawns by cutting a line down the back of each one, through the shell from the base of the head to the top of the tail. Pull out the black line of intestine from each one. Clean the mussels under cold water, pulling off any hairy or stringy bits. Hasselback the squid in the same way you did the potatoes.

STEP 3

Cut each corn cob into four pieces – the easiest way to do this is by positioning your knife, covering it with a tea towel and hitting it with a rolling pin. Add the corn to the tray, toss in the oil and return to the oven for 5 mins.

STEP 4

Mash together the butter, parsley, paprika, garlic and lemon zest. Stuff some of the butter into the back of each prawn and inside the squids. Turn the oven up to 220C/200C fan/gas 6. Add the seafood, lemon wedges and chorizo to the pan and toss everything together. Dot the remaining butter over the top, season well and return to the oven for 10 mins. If any of the prawns haven't turned pink or any mussels haven't opened, move them around the pan to the hot spots, then return to the oven for another 2-3 mins. Remove and discard any mussels which haven't opened. Scatter some parsley over and serve.

Christmas dinner for one

Prep:35 mins **Cook:**45 mins

Serves 1

Ingredients

- 3 pork chipolatas
- 1 small apple , cored, ½ grated, ½ cut into wedges
- 3 pecans , chopped
- 2 slices white bread , chopped into small pieces
- pinch of dried sage
- 1 skinless chicken breast
- 4 rashers streaky bacon
- 5 Brussels sprouts , trimmed
- 2 small potatoes , quartered
- 1 medium parsnip , trimmed

To serve

- 1-2 tbsp pickled red cabbage

- 1 garlic clove , sliced
- 3 bay leaves
- 2 tbsp vegetable or sunflower oil
- 250ml milk
- 2 cloves
- 1 shallot
- 2 tsp butter
- 1 tbsp balsamic vinegar
- 250ml red wine
- 250ml beef or chicken stock (can be made with 1/2 stock cube)

- 1 tsp cranberry sauce

Method

STEP 1

Heat the oven to 200C/180C fan/gas 6. Squeeze the meat from one of the chipolatas into a bowl, discarding the skin. Put the grated apple in a clean tea towel and squeeze out any excess liquid, then add to the sausagemeat with the pecans, a quarter of the bread and the sage. Season, then combine using your hands and form into a fat sausage shape. Cut a long slit in the chicken breast lengthways on one side, being careful not to cut it in half (you should be able to open it up like a book). Stuff the chicken breast with the stuffing sausage, then wrap two of the bacon rashers around it so it's fully enclosed, securing it with a couple of cocktail sticks.

STEP 2

Put the stuffed chicken breast in a large roasting tin. Wrap the remaining bacon rashers around the remaining chipolatas and add to the tin around the chicken.

STEP 3

Add the apple wedges, sprouts and potatoes to the roasting tin. Cut the parsnip in half lengthways and put it, cut-side down, on a chopping board. Make very thin, close cuts into the parsnip halves that go almost but not fully through – put a wooden spoon on either side of the parsnip halves to stop the knife going through, if you like. Transfer to the roasting tin with the garlic and two of the bay leaves. Drizzle over the oil and season everything with salt and pepper. Roast for 40-45 mins, or until everything is cooked through. Brush the vegetables in the oil and meat juices once or twice near the end of the cooking time.

STEP 4

Meanwhile, pour the milk into a small saucepan with the remaining bay leaf, the cloves and shallot. Heat gently for 5-6 mins, stirring occasionally, or until the shallot is starting to soften. Strain the milk into a heatproof jug, reserving the shallot and discarding the bay leaf and cloves. Return the milk to the pan with the remaining bread and cook, stirring, until you have a thick, porridge-like sauce. Add half the butter and stir until melted, then season, remove from the heat and set aside.

STEP 5

Slice the reserved shallot, then add to a deep frying pan with the rest of the butter. Fry until just golden, then pour in the balsamic vinegar. Continue to cook until the vinegar has reduced and is thick and sticky, then add the wine. Cook until the wine has reduced by half, then stir in the stock and bubble until the sauce is glossy and slightly thickened.

STEP 6

Gently reheat the bread sauce. Slice half the chicken (reserving the rest for leftovers) and put on a plate with the pigs in blankets and the roast apple, sprouts, potatoes and parsnip. Drizzle over the red wine gravy and serve with the pickled red cabbage and cranberry and bread sauces on the side.

Potted crab

Prep:10 mins **Cook:**2 mins

Serves 2

Ingredients

- 150g picked white crabmeat , the freshest you can buy
- 2 tbsp mayonnaise
- 1 shallot , peeled and finely chopped

For the paprika butter

- 60g butter

- small handful chives , chopped
- ½ orange , zested
- 2 large slices sourdough , grilled or griddled, to serve

- ¼ tsp smoked paprika

Method

STEP 1

Tip the crabmeat into a bowl and mix with the mayonnaise, shallot, chives, orange zest and some seasoning. Spoon the mixture into a shallow serving dish. Smooth the top over, then pop in the fridge to chill.

STEP 2

Gently melt the butter and smoked paprika together. Leave the butter to cool a little, but don't let it solidify. Carefully pour the clear butter fat over the crab, leaving the milky butter residue still in the saucepan. Return to the fridge for 20-25 mins or up to a day to firm the butter up. Serve with some grilled sourdough for spreading everything over.

Ultimate apple pie

Total time2 hrs and 30 mins Ready in 2½ hours

Serves 8

Ingredients

For the filling

- 1kg Bramley apples
- 140g golden caster sugar

For the pastry

- 225g butter, room temperature
- 50g golden caster sugar, plus extra
- 2 eggs

- ½ tsp cinnamon
- 3 tbsp flour

- 350g plain flour, preferably organic
- softly whipped cream, to serve

Method

STEP 1

Put a layer of paper towels on a large baking sheet. Quarter, core, peel and slice the apples about 5mm thick and lay evenly on the baking sheet. Put paper towels on top and set aside while you make and chill the pastry.

STEP 2

For the pastry, beat the butter and sugar in a large bowl until just mixed. Break in a whole egg and a yolk (keep the white for glazing later). Beat together for just under 1 min – it will look a bit like scrambled egg. Now work in the flour with a wooden spoon, a third at a time, until it's beginning to clump up, then finish gathering it together with your hands. Gently work the dough into a ball, wrap in cling film, and chill for 45 mins. Now mix the 140g/5oz sugar, the cinnamon and flour for the filling in a bowl that is large enough to take the apples later.

STEP 3

After the pastry has chilled, heat the oven to 190C/fan 170C/gas 5. Lightly beat the egg white with a fork. Cut off a third of the pastry and keep it wrapped while you roll out the rest, and use this to line a pie tin – 20-22cm round and 4cm deep – leaving a slight overhang. Roll the remaining third to a circle about 28cm in diameter. Pat the apples dry with kitchen paper, and tip them into the bowl with the cinnamon-sugar mix. Give a quick mix with your hands and immediately pile high into the pastry-lined tin.

STEP 4

Brush a little water around the pastry rim and lay the pastry lid over the apples pressing the edges together to seal. Trim the edge with a sharp knife and make 5 little slashes on top of the lid for the steam to escape. (Can be frozen at this stage.) Brush it all with the egg white and sprinkle with caster sugar. Bake for 40-45 mins, until golden, then remove and let it sit for 5-10 mins. Sprinkle with more sugar and serve while still warm from the oven with softly whipped cream.

One-pan roast butter chicken

Prep: 30 mins **Cook:** 1 hr and 10 mins

Serves 4

Ingredients

- 1 lemon , halved
- 1 medium chicken

For the curry butter

- 100g soft unsalted butter
- 2 garlic cloves , crushed
- small piece ginger , finely grated
- 1 tsp garam masala
- 1 tsp turmeric
- 1 tsp ground cloves
- handful coriander leaves , chopped

For the sauce

- 3 garlic cloves , finely grated
- small piece ginger , finely grated
- 4 cardamom pods
- 4 cloves
- 1 tsp fennel seeds
- 2 tsp garam masala
- 1 tsp hot chilli powder
- 2 tsp turmeric
- 500ml passata
- 200ml double cream

Method

STEP 1

Heat oven to 220C/200C fan/gas 7. Put the lemon halves in the chicken cavity. Stir all the ingredients for the curry butter together and season with salt and lots of pepper. Use your fingers to stuff the curry butter under the skin and smear it all over the meat.

STEP 2

Place the chicken in a flameproof roasting tin, on a trivet, if you have one. Roast for 20 mins, then turn the oven down to 180C/160C/gas 4. Continue to roast for 40 mins, or until the chicken is cooked through. Remove the chicken from the tin and leave to rest while you make the sauce.

STEP 3

If your roasting tin is flameproof, place it directly on the heat, if not, scrape all the buttery goodness from the tin into a saucepan and set over a low heat to make the sauce. Gently sweat

84

the garlic and ginger in the curry butter. Scatter in the cardamom, cloves and fennel seeds and cook for 2 mins, then add the ground spices and cook for another 2 mins. Pour in the passata and gently reduce by half before adding the cream and reducing by a third. To finish the sauce, pour in the resting juices, season and add a squeeze of the roasted lemon from the cavity of the chicken. Carve the chicken and serve with the sauce.

Smoky sausage casserole

Prep:15 mins **Cook:**1 hr

Serves 4

Ingredients

- 1 tbsp olive oil
- 1 onion, finely chopped
- 1 garlic clove, crushed
- 1 large celery stick, finely chopped
- 2 peppers (any colour), cut into chunks
- pack 6 pork sausage (about 400g/14oz)
- 1 tsp sweet smoked paprika
- ½ tsp ground cumin

- ½ tsp chilli flakes
- 2 x 400g cans chopped tomatoes
- 400g can cannellini beans, drained
- 250g bag spinach (or use the same quantity as frozen)
- 2 tbsp fresh breadcrumbs (or frozen with herbs)

Method

STEP 1

Put the oil in a large, heatproof casserole dish over a medium heat and add the onion, cooking for 5 mins until starting to soften. Tip in the garlic, celery and peppers, and give everything a good stir. Cook for 5 mins more.

STEP 2

Turn the heat to high and add the sausages. Cook for a few mins until browned all over, then reduce the heat to medium, sprinkle in the spices and season well. Pour over the tomatoes and bring to a simmer. Cover and continue simmering gently for 40 mins, stirring every now and then.

STEP 3

Heat the grill to high and uncover the casserole. Add the beans and spinach, and stir to warm through. Scatter over the breadcrumbs and grill for 2-3 mins until golden and crisp.

Slow-cooker beef pot roast

Prep: 15 mins **Cook:** 7 hrs and 30 mins

Serves 6 - 8

Ingredients

- 2 tbsp sunflower oil
- 1½ kg rolled beef brisket
- 2 tbsp plain flour
- 3 carrots, chopped
- 3 sticks of celery, chopped
- 2 parsnips, chopped
- 1 onion, chopped

- 80g button mushrooms
- 2 bay leaves
- 2 garlic cloves, crushed
- 2 tsp English mustard
- 500ml red wine
- 250ml beef stock

Method

STEP 1

Heat 2 tbsp sunflower oil in a large pan. Dust 1½ kg rolled beef brisket with 2 tbsp plain flour and season well with salt and pepper.

STEP 2

Put 3 chopped carrots, 3 chopped celery sticks, 2 chopped parsnips, 1 chopped onion and 80g button mushrooms in the bottom of your slow cooker and turn it to Low.

STEP 3

Sear the beef all over in the hot pan then place it on top of the vegetables in the slow cooker.

STEP 4

Add the 2 bay leaves, 2 crushed garlic cloves and 2 tsp English mustard then pour over 500ml red wine and 250ml beef stock. Cover with the lid and cook for 7 hours.

STEP 5

Heat oven to 200C/180C fan/gas 6. Carefully take the beef out of the slow cooker and place it on a baking tray then roast it in the oven for 20 mins.

STEP 6

While the beef is in the oven, carefully ladle the cooking liquid out of the slow cooker into a shallow pan. Boil rapidly on a high heat to reduce to a rich gravy.

STEP 7

Serve the beef sliced with roast potatoes, the softened vegetables, gravy and wilted greens, if you like.

Honey mustard chicken pot with parsnips

Prep:5 mins **Cook:**40 mins

Serves 4

Ingredients

- 1 tbsp olive oil
- 8 bone-in chicken thighs, skin removed
- 2 onions, finely chopped
- 350g parsnip, cut into sticks
- 300ml vegetable stock

- 2 tbsp wholegrain mustard
- 2 tbsp clear honey
- few thyme sprigs
- flat-leaf parsley, to serve (optional)

Method

STEP 1

Heat half the oil in a large frying pan or shallow casserole with a lid. Brown the chicken until golden, then set aside. Heat the remaining oil, then cook the onions for 5 mins until softened.

STEP 2

Nestle the thighs back amongst the onions and add the parnips. Mix the stock with the mustard and honey, then pour in. Scatter over the thyme, then bring to a simmer. Cover, then cook for 30 mins (or longer, see tip) until the chicken is tender, then season. Serve with steamed greens.

Home-style chicken curry

Prep:15 mins **Cook:**30 mins

Serves 4

Ingredients

- 1 large onion
- 6 garlic cloves, roughly chopped
- 50g ginger, roughly chopped
- 4 tbsp vegetable oil
- 2 tsp cumin seeds
- 1 tsp fennel seeds
- 5cm cinnamon stick
- 1 tsp chilli flakes

- 1 tsp garam masala
- 1 tsp turmeric
- 1 tsp caster sugar
- 400g can chopped tomatoes
- 8 chicken thighs, skinned, boneless (about 800g)
- 250ml hot chicken stock
- 2 tbsp chopped coriander

Method

STEP 1

Roughly chop 1 large onion, transfer to a small food processor, and add 3 tbsp of water - process to a slack paste. You could use a stick blender for this or coarsely grate the onion into a bowl – there's no need to add any water if you are grating the onion. Tip into a small bowl and leave on one side.

STEP 2

Put 6 roughly chopped garlic cloves and 50g roughly chopped ginger into the same food processor and add 4 tbsp water – process until smooth and spoon into another small bowl. Alternatively, crush the garlic to a paste with a knife or garlic press and finely grate the ginger.

STEP 3

Heat 4 tbsp vegetable oil in a wok or sturdy pan set over a medium heat.

STEP 4

Combine 2 tsp cumin seeds and 1 tsp fennel seeds with a 5cm cinnamon stick and 1 tsp chilli flakes and add to the pan in one go. Swirl everything around for about 30 secs until the spices release a fragrant aroma.

STEP 5

Add the onion paste – it will splutter in the beginning. Fry until the water evaporates and the onions turn a lovely dark golden - this should take about 7-8 mins.

STEP 6

Add the garlic and ginger paste and cook for another 2 mins – stirring all the time.

STEP 7

Stir in 1 tsp garam masala, 1 tsp turmeric, and 1 tsp caster sugar and continue cooking for 20 secs before tipping in a 400g can chopped tomatoes.

STEP 8

Continue cooking on a medium heat for about 10 mins without a lid until the tomatoes reduce and darken.

STEP 9

Cut 8 skinless, boneless chicken thighs into 3cm chunks and add to the pan once the tomatoes have thickened to a paste.

STEP 10

Cook for 5 mins to coat the chicken in the masala and seal in the juices, and then pour over 250ml hot chicken stock.

STEP 11

Simmer for 8-10 mins without a lid until the chicken is tender and the masala lightly thickened – you might need to add an extra ladleful of stock or water if the curry needs it.

STEP 12

Sprinkle with 2 tbsp chopped coriander and serve with Indian flatbreads or fluffy basmati rice and a pot of yogurt on the side.

Spiced chicken, spinach & sweet potato stew

Prep: 15 mins **Cook:** 40 mins

Serves 4

Ingredients

- 3 sweet potatoes, cut into chunks
- 190g bag spinach
- 1 tbsp sunflower oil

For the spice paste

- 2 onions, chopped
- 1 red chilli, chopped
- 1 tsp paprika
- thumb-sized piece ginger, grated

To serve

- pumpkin seeds, toasted
- 2-3 preserved lemons, deseeded and chopped

- 8 chicken thighs, skinless and boneless
- 500ml chicken stock

- 400g can tomatoes
- 2 preserved lemons, deseeded and chopped

- 4 naan bread, warmed

Method

STEP 1

Put the sweet potato in a large, deep saucepan over a high heat. Cover with boiling water and boil for 10 mins. Meanwhile, put all the paste ingredients in a food processor and blend until very finely chopped. Set aside until needed.

STEP 2

Put the spinach in a large colander in the sink and pour the sweet potatoes and their cooking water over it to drain the potatoes and wilt the spinach at the same time. Leave to steam-dry.

STEP 3

Return the saucepan to the heat (no need to wash it first), then add the oil, followed by the spice paste. Fry the paste for about 5 mins until thickened, then add the chicken. Fry for 8-10 mins until the chicken starts to colour. Pour over the stock, bring to the boil and leave to simmer for 10 mins, stirring occasionally.

STEP 4

Check the chicken is cooked by cutting into one of the thighs and making sure it's white throughout with no signs of pink. Season with black pepper, then add the sweet potato. Leave to simmer for a further 5 mins. Meanwhile, roughly chop the spinach and add to the stew. *At this point you can leave the stew to cool and freeze for up to 3 months, if you like.*

STEP 5

Scatter over the pumpkin seeds and preserved lemons, and serve with warm naan bread on the side.

Spanish meatball & butter bean stew

Prep: 15 mins **Cook:** 35 mins

Serves 3

Ingredients

- 350g lean pork mince
- 2 tsp olive oil
- 1 large red onion, chopped
- 2 peppers, sliced, any colour will do
- 3 garlic cloves, crushed
- 1 tbsp sweet smoked paprika

- 2 x 400g cans chopped tomatoes
- 400g can butter beans, drained
- 2 tsp golden caster sugar
- small bunch parsley, chopped
- crusty bread, to serve (optional)

Method

STEP 1

Season the pork, working the seasoning in with your hands, then shape into small meatballs. Heat the oil in a large pan, add the meatballs and cook for 5 mins, until golden brown all over. Push to one side of the pan and add the onion and peppers. Cook for a further 5 mins, stirring now and then, until the veg has softened, then stir in the garlic and paprika. Stir everything around in the pan for 1 min, then add the tomatoes. Cover with a lid and simmer for 10 mins.

STEP 2

Uncover, stir in the beans, the sugar and some seasoning, then simmer for a further 10 mins, uncovered. Just before serving, stir in the parsley. Serve with crusty bread for dunking, if you like.

Coconut fish curry

Prep: 15 mins **Cook:** 15 mins

Serves 4

Ingredients

- 1 tbsp vegetable oil
- 1 onion, finely chopped
- thumb-sized piece ginger, finely grated
- 3 garlic cloves, crushed
- 1 tsp shrimp paste
- 1 small red chilli, shredded (deseeded if you don't like it too hot)
- 2 lemongrass stalks, split, then bruised with a rolling pin
- 1 heaped tbsp medium curry powder
- cooked rice, to serve

- 1 heaped tbsp light muscovado sugar
- small bunch coriander, stems finely chopped
- 400g can coconut milk
- 450g skinless hake fillets, cut into rectangles, roughly credit card size
- 220g pack frozen raw whole prawns (we used Big & Juicy Tiger Prawns, which are sustainably fished)
- 1 lime, halved

Method

STEP 1

Heat the oil in a wide, lidded frying pan, then soften the onion for 5 mins. Increase the heat a little, stir in the ginger, garlic, shrimp paste, chilli and lemongrass, and cook for 2 mins. Add the curry powder and sugar, and keep stirring. When the sugar starts to melt and everything starts to clump together, add the coriander stems, coconut milk and 2 tbsp water, then bring to a simmer.

STEP 2

Add the fish to the sauce, tuck the prawns in here and there, then squeeze over half the lime. Pop on the lid and simmer for 5 mins more or until the hake is just cooked and flaking, and the prawns are pink through. Taste for seasoning, adding a squeeze more lime to the sauce if you like. Scatter over the coriander leaves and serve with rice.

Chicken & chorizo rice pot

Prep: 20 mins **Cook:** 1 hr and 20 mins

Serves 4

Ingredients

- 1 tbsp oil
- 8 chicken pieces or 1 whole chicken, jointed
- 1 large onion, chopped
- 1 red pepper, deseeded and chopped into large chunks
- 3 garlic cloves, crushed
- 225g chorizo, skinned and sliced
- 1 tbsp tomato purée
- 1 tbsp thyme leaf, chopped
- 150ml white wine
- 850ml chicken stock
- 400g long grain rice
- 2 tbsp chopped parsley

Method

STEP 1

Heat the oil in a large flameproof casserole dish and brown the chicken pieces on all sides – you may have to do this in batches. Remove from the dish and put to one side.

STEP 2

Lower the heat, add the onion and pepper, and gently cook for 10 mins until softened. Add the garlic and chorizo, and cook for a further 2 mins until the chorizo has released some of its oils into the dish. Stir in the tomato purée and cook for 1 min more.

STEP 3

Return the chicken pieces to the dish along with the thyme, white wine and stock. Bring the liquid to a boil, cover the dish with a tight-fitting lid and lower the heat. Cook for 30 mins.

STEP 4

Tip in the rice and stir everything together. Cover, set over a low heat and cook for a further 15 mins, or until the rice is cooked and has absorbed most of the cooking liquid. Remove from the heat and leave the dish to sit for 10 mins to absorb any remaining liquid. Season to taste and scatter with parsley to serve.

Spring chicken in a pot

Prep: 20 mins **Cook:** 45 mins

Serves 4

Ingredients

- 1 tbsp olive oil
- 1 onion , chopped
- 500g boneless, skinless chicken thigh
- 300g small new potato
- 425ml low-salt vegetable stock (such as Kallo low-salt vegetable stock cubes)
- 350g broccoli , cut into small florets
- 350g spring green , shredded
- 140g petits pois
- bunch spring onion , sliced
- 2 tbsp pesto

Method

STEP 1

Heat the oil in a large, heavy pan. Add the onion, gently fry for 5 mins until softened, add the chicken, then fry until lightly coloured. Add the potatoes, stock and plenty of freshly ground black pepper, then bring to the boil. Cover, then simmer for 30 mins until the potatoes are tender and the chicken is cooked. Can be frozen at this point.

STEP 2

Add the broccoli, spring greens, petit pois and spring onions, stir well, then return to the boil. Cover, then cook for 5 mins more, stir in the pesto and heat through.

Easter chocolate pots with pick 'n' mix toppings

Prep: 10 mins **Cook:** 5 mins

plus 2-3 hrs chilling

Serves 6

Ingredients

- 500g fresh custard
- ½ tsp ground cinnamon
- 200g dark chocolate , chopped into small pieces

- 100g crème fraîche
- mixture of crushed chocolate mini eggs, chopped toasted hazelnuts and sprinkles, to serve

Method

STEP 1

Heat the custard with the cinnamon in a saucepan until just simmering. Remove from the heat, add the chocolate, stir until melted, then fold in the crème fraîche.

STEP 2

Divide the mixture between six ramekins or teacups, or tip into one large dish. Transfer to the fridge to chill for 2-3 hrs, or until set. Put the mini eggs, hazelnuts and sprinkles in separate small bowls and serve with the chocolate pots for everyone to top as they like.

Lamb shank Madras

Prep: 40 mins **Cook:** 4 hrs

Serves 4

Ingredients

- 4 tbsp natural yogurt
- 1 tbsp ground cumin
- 1 tsp turmeric
- 4 lamb shanks
- 2 tbsp sunflower oil
- 4 onions , sliced
- 4 tbsp Madras curry powder
- 8 garlic cloves , grated or crushed
- thumb-sized piece ginger , grated
- 220g tin chopped tomatoes
- 3 whole dried red chillies
- 5 curry leaves
- 4 cardamom pods , split
- 3 tbsp lime pickle
- 300ml chicken stock
- chopped mint leaves, naan bread and rice, to serve

Method

STEP 1

Tip the yogurt, cumin, turmeric, 1 tsp sea salt and the lamb shanks into a large mixing bowl, then mix to coat the lamb. Cover and pop in the fridge for a couple of hrs, or overnight if you have time.

STEP 2

Heat oven to 160C/140C fan/gas 4. Heat the oil in a large flameproof casserole dish over a medium heat, add the shanks and brown all over for 10 mins, then remove from the dish. Scatter the onions into the dish and fry for 10 mins until golden brown. Stir in the curry powder, garlic and ginger and cook for 3 mins until aromatic. Add the lamb shanks back to the dish along with the tomatoes, chillies, curry leaves, cardamom pods and lime pickle. Give everything a good stir and pour over the stock. Bring up to a simmer, cover, then transfer to the oven and cook for 3 hrs.

STEP 3

Remove the lid and cook for 1 hr more – this will help reduce some of the liquid and char any exposed meat. When the lamb is very tender, leave to rest for 30 mins or leave to cool completely and reheat the next day for the best flavour. (Can be made up to two days in advance.) Scatter with chopped mint and serve with naan bread and rice on the side.

All-in–one chicken with wilted spinach

Prep:20 mins **Cook:**1 hr

Serves 2

Ingredients

- 2 beetroot , peeled and cut into small chunks
- 300g celeriac , cut into small chunks
- 2 red onions , quartered
- 8 garlic cloves , 4 crushed, the rest left whole, but peeled
- 1 tbsp rapeseed oil
- 1½ tbsp fresh thyme leaves , plus extra to serve

- 1 lemon , zested and juiced
- 1 tsp fennel seeds
- 1 tsp English mustard powder
- 1 tsp smoked paprika
- 4 tbsp bio yogurt
- 4 bone-in chicken thighs , skin removed
- 260g bag spinach

Method

STEP 1

Heat oven to 200C/180C fan/gas 6. Tip the beetroot, celeriac, onions and whole garlic cloves into a shallow roasting tin. Add the oil, 1 tbsp thyme, half the lemon zest, fennel seeds and a squeeze of lemon juice, then toss together. Roast for 20 mins while you prepare the chicken.

STEP 2

Stir the mustard powder and paprika into 2 tbsp yogurt in a bowl. Add half the crushed garlic, the remaining lemon zest and thyme, and juice from half the lemon. Add the chicken and toss well until it's coated all over. Put the chicken in the tin with the veg and roast for 40 mins until the chicken is cooked through and the vegetables are tender.

STEP 3

About 5 mins before the chicken is ready, wash and drain the spinach and put it in a pan with the remaining crushed garlic. Cook until wilted, then turn off the heat and stir in the remaining yogurt. Scatter some extra thyme over the chicken and vegetables, then serve.

Prawn laksa curry bowl

Prep:5 mins **Cook:**10 mins

Serves 2

Ingredients

- 1 tbsp olive oil
- 1 red chilli , finely sliced
- 2 ½ tbsp Thai red curry paste
- 1 vegetable stock cube
- 400ml can reduced fat coconut milk
- 2 tsp fish sauce

- 100g rice noodles
- 2 limes , juice of 1, the other halved
- 150g cooked king prawns
- ½ small pack coriander , roughly chopped

Method

STEP 1

Heat the oil in a medium saucepan and add the chilli. Cook for 1 min, then add the curry paste, stir and cook for 1 min more. Dissolve the stock cube in a large jug in 700ml boiling water, then pour into the pan and stir to combine. Tip in the coconut milk and bring to the boil.

STEP 2

Add the fish sauce and a little seasoning. Toss in the noodles and cook for a further 3-4 mins until softening. Squeeze in the lime juice, add the prawns and cook through until warm, about 2-3 mins. Scatter over some of the coriander.

STEP 3

Serve in bowls with the remaining coriander and lime wedges on top for squeezing over.

One-pan egg & veg brunch

Prep:5 mins **Cook:**25 mins

Serves 2 adults + 2 children

Ingredients

- 300g baby new potatoes , halved
- ½ tbsp rapeseed oil
- 1 knob of butter
- 1 courgette , cut into small chunks
- 1 yellow pepper , cut into small chunks
- toast , to serve

- 1 red pepper , cut into small chunks
- 2 spring onions , finely sliced
- 1 garlic clove , crushed
- 1 sprig thyme , leaves picked
- 4 eggs

Method

STEP 1

Boil the new potatoes for 8 mins, then drain.

STEP 2

Heat the oil and butter in a large non-stick frying pan, then add the courgette, peppers, potatoes and a little salt and pepper. Cook for 10 mins, stirring from time to time until everything is starting to brown. Add the spring onions, garlic and thyme and cook for 2 mins more.

STEP 3

Make four spaces in the pan and crack in the eggs. Cover with foil or a lid and cook for around 4 mins, or until the eggs are cooked (with the yolks soft for dipping into). Sprinkle with more thyme leaves and ground black pepper if you like. Serve with toast.

Beer-braised brisket pot roast

Prep:5 mins **Cook:**3 hrs - 5 hrs

Serves 6

Ingredients

- 1 beef stock cube , crushed
- 1 tsp dried tarragon
- 2 tsp cracked black pepper
- 2kg rolled beef brisket
- 1 tbsp sunflower oil
- 500-550ml bottle of dark ale

- 2 tbsp beef extract
- 1 tbsp muscovado sugar
- 2 tbsp dried onion flakes
- 500ml beef stock
- long-stem broccoli , to serve (optional)

Method

STEP 1

Heat the oven to 150C/130C fan/gas 2. Mix the stock cube with the tarragon and pepper in a small bowl. Rub over the brisket and season. Heat the oil in a large flameproof casserole dish or roasting tin over a medium-high heat, add the brisket and brown well on all sides.

STEP 2

Stir in the ale and beef extract, then tip in the sugar and onion flakes and add enough of the beef stock to come two-thirds of the way up the sides of the brisket. Bring to the boil, cover and roast in the oven for 3 hrs, checking every 30 mins to see if the brisket is tender (but you may need to roast it for up to 5 hrs). Transfer the brisket to a board and leave to rest for 15 mins. Slice and serve with the stock spooned over and some steamed long stem broccoli on the side, if you like.

Simple fish stew

Prep:10 mins **Cook:**20 mins - 25 mins

Serves 2

Ingredients

- 1 tbsp olive oil
- 1 tsp fennel seeds

- 2 carrots, diced
- 2 celery sticks, diced

- 2 garlic cloves, finely chopped
- 2 leeks, thinly sliced
- 400g can chopped tomatoes
- 500ml hot fish stock, heated to a simmer

- 2 skinless pollock fillets (about 200g), thawed if frozen, and cut into chunks
- 85g raw shelled king prawns

Method

STEP 1

Heat the oil in a large pan, add the fennel seeds, carrots, celery and garlic, and cook for 5 mins until starting to soften. Tip in the leeks, tomatoes and stock, season and bring to the boil, then cover and simmer for 15-20 mins until the vegetables are tender and the sauce has thickened and reduced slightly.

STEP 2

Add the fish, scatter over the prawns and cook for 2 mins more until lightly cooked. Ladle into bowls and serve with a spoon.

Butter bean, mushroom & bacon pot pies

Prep:15 mins **Cook:**50 mins

Serves 4

Ingredients

- 3 tbsp rapeseed oil
- 2 red onions , thinly sliced
- 500g mushrooms , thickly sliced
- 70g smoked streaky bacon , sliced into thin strips
- 2 tbsp plain flour
- 500ml low-salt vegetable stock

- 250g kale , roughly sliced
- 3 tsp wholegrain mustard
- 2 tbsp reduced-fat crème fraîche
- 1 tbsp finely chopped tarragon
- 1 lemon , zested and juiced
- 2 x 400g cans butter beans , drained and rinsed

Method

STEP 1

Heat 2 tbsp of the oil in a saucepan or large flameproof casserole dish. Fry the onions for 10 mins until soft, then add the mushrooms and bacon and fry for another 5 mins until golden. Stir in the flour and cook for 2 mins more. Gradually pour in the stock, then bring to the boil and bubble for 2 mins. Add the kale and cook for another 5 mins, then stir in the mustard, crème fraîche, half the tarragon and the lemon juice. Spoon the mushroom mixture into four small baking dishes.

STEP 2

Heat the oven to 180C/160C fan/gas 4. Put the butter beans in a food processor with the remaining oil and tarragon and the lemon zest. Blitz until chunky, adding 2-3 tbsp water to loosen if needed.

STEP 3

Spoon the butter bean mixture over the filling, smoothing with the back of a spoon. Bake for 20-25 mins until golden. Leave to cool slightly, then serve.

Sausage & bean casserole

Prep: 15 mins **Cook:** 1 hr

Serves 4 - 6

Ingredients

- 2 tbsp olive or rapeseed oil
- 1 onion, finely chopped
- 2 medium sticks celery, finely chopped
- 1 yellow pepper, chopped
- 1 red pepper, chopped
- 6 cooking chorizo sausages (about 400g)
- 6 pork sausages (about 400g)
- 3 fat garlic cloves, chopped
- 1 ½ tsp sweet smoked paprika
- ½ tsp ground cumin

- 1 tbsp dried thyme
- 125ml white wine
- 2 x 400g cans cherry tomatoes or chopped tomatoes
- 2 sprigs fresh thyme
- 1 chicken stock cube
- 1 x 400g can aduki beans, drained and rinsed
- 1 bunch chives, snipped (optional)

Method

STEP 1

Heat 2 tbsp olive or rapeseed oil in a large heavy-based pan.

STEP 2

Add 1 finely chopped onion and cook gently for 5 minutes.

STEP 3

Add 2 finely chopped medium celery sticks, 1 chopped yellow pepper and 1 chopped red pepper and cook for a further 5 mins.

STEP 4

Add 6 chorizo sausages and 6 pork sausages and fry for 5 minutes.

STEP 5

Stir in 3 chopped garlic cloves, 1 ½ tsp sweet smoked paprika, ½ tsp ground cumin and 1 tbsp dried thyme and continue cooking for 1 – 2 mins or until the aromas are released.

STEP 6

Pour in 125ml white wine and use a wooden spoon to remove any residue stuck to the pan.

STEP 7

Add two 400g cans of tomatoes, and 2 sprigs of fresh thyme and bring to a simmer. Crumble in the chicken stock cube and stir.

STEP 8

Cook for 40 minutes. Stir in a 400g drained and rinsed can of aduki beans and cook for a further five minutes.

STEP 9

Remove the thyme sprigs, season with black pepper and stir through some snipped chives, if using. Serve.

Peri-peri chicken pilaf

Prep:20 mins **Cook:**40 mins

Serves 4

Ingredients

- 1 tbsp olive oil

- pack of 6 skinless boneless chicken thighs , cut into large chunks
- 2 tbsp peri-peri seasoning
- 1 onion , finely chopped
- 2 garlic cloves , crushed
- 350g basmati rice
- 500ml hot chicken stock
- 3 peppers (any colour you like), sliced into strips
- 3 large tomatoes , deseeded and roughly chopped
- small pack parsley , roughly chopped
- 2 red chillies , sliced (optional)
- ½ lemon , cut into wedges, to serve

Method

STEP 1

Heat the oil in a large pan over a medium heat. Rub the chicken with 1 tbsp of the peri-peri and brown in the pan for 1 min each side until golden. Transfer to a plate and set aside.

STEP 2

Add the onion to the pan and cook on a gentle heat for 8-10 mins until soft. Add the garlic and remaining peri-peri, and give everything a stir. Tip in the rice and stir to coat.

STEP 3

Add the stock and return the chicken to the pan. Add the peppers and cover with a lid, then simmer gently for 25 mins until cooked. About 5 mins before the end of cooking, add the tomatoes.

STEP 4

Stir through the parsley, scatter over the chillies (if you like it spicy) and serve with lemon wedges.

Penang prawn & pineapple curry

Prep:25 mins **Cook:**40 mins

Serves 8, with other dishes

Ingredients

For the toasted coconut

- 100g fresh coconut flesh
- 2 tsp sunflower oil

103

For the curry

- thumb-sized piece ginger , peeled
- 6 garlic cloves , peeled
- 1 ½ tbsp mild curry powder
- 100ml sunflower oil
- 7 curry leaves
- 1 cinnamon stick
- 1 star anise
- 3 cardamom pods
- 6 cloves
- 6 shallots , thinly sliced lengthways
- 3 tbsp tamarind paste
- 1 pineapple , peeled, cored and cut into chunks
- 1 tbsp palm sugar or soft brown sugar
- 400ml can full-fat thick coconut milk
- 24 large raw king prawns , peeled
- handful coriander leaves and cooked white or brown rice, to serve

Method

STEP 1

Finely grate the coconut, then toast slowly in a wok, stirring until evenly dark brown (it will start to smell very strong, but it will work a treat). While it's still warm, pound to a paste with the sunflower oil using a pestle and mortar. Set aside.

STEP 2

Finely grate or pound the ginger and garlic together using a pestle and mortar. Make a loose curry paste by adding 75ml water to the curry powder. Heat the oil in the wok until it's just starting to smoke, then throw in the curry leaves, cinnamon stick, star anise, cardamom pods and cloves and cook for 1 min until fragrant.

STEP 3

Add the shallots and ginger and garlic paste, cook for around 7 mins until softened and starting to brown, then add the curry powder paste. This is the most important part of making the curry. Ideally, cook over a very low heat and wait until the oil separates and bubbles over the paste, around 10-12 mins. Scrape the bottom of the pan occasionally to remove the crust.

STEP 4

When the oil has come to the top, add the tamarind paste, pineapple and sugar. Pour in the coconut milk. When the mixture starts boiling, add the prawns and return to the boil, then stir through the toasted coconut. Season the curry with salt, scatter over the coriander and serve with rice.

One-pan spaghetti with nduja, fennel & olives

Prep: 15 mins **Cook:** 15 mins

Serves 4

Ingredients

- 400g spaghetti
- 3 garlic cloves , very thinly sliced
- ½ fennel , halved and very thinly sliced
- 75g nduja or sobrasada paste (see tip)
- 200g tomatoes (the best you can get), chopped into chunks
- 75g black olives , pitted and sliced
- 2 tsp tomato purée
- 3 tbsp olive oil , plus a drizzle
- 2 tsp red wine vinegar
- 40g pecorino , plus extra to serve
- handful basil , torn

Method

STEP 1

Boil the kettle. Put all the ingredients except the pecorino and basil in a wide saucepan or deep frying pan and season well. Pour over 800ml kettle-hot water and bring to a simmer, using your tongs to ease the spaghetti under the liquid as it starts to soften.

STEP 2

Simmer, uncovered, for 10-12 mins, tossing the spaghetti through the liquid every so often until it is cooked and the sauce is reduced and clinging to it. Add a splash more hot water if the sauce is too thick or does not cover the pasta while it cooks. Turn up the heat for the final few mins to drive off the excess liquid, leaving you with a rich sauce. Stir through the pecorino and basil, and serve with an extra drizzle of oil and pecorino on the side.

Fruity lamb tagine

Prep: 15 mins **Cook:** 1 hr and 30 mins

Serves 4

Ingredients

- 2 tbsp olive oil
- 500g lean diced lamb
- 1 large onion, roughly chopped

105

- 2 large carrots, quartered lengthways and cut into chunks
- 2 garlic cloves, finely chopped
- 2 tbsp ras-el-hanout spice mix

- 400g can chopped tomato
- 400g can chickpea, rinsed and drained
- 200g dried apricot
- 600ml chicken stock

To serve

- 120g pack pomegranate seeds

- 2 large handfuls coriander, roughly chopped

Method

STEP 1

Heat oven to 180C/160C fan/gas 4. Heat the oil in a casserole and brown the lamb on all sides. Scoop the lamb out onto a plate, then add the onion and carrots and cook for 2-3 mins until golden. Add the garlic and cook for 1 min more. Stir in the spices and tomatoes, and season. Tip the lamb back in with the chickpeas and apricots. Pour over the stock, stir and bring to a simmer. Cover the dish and place in the oven for 1 hr.

STEP 2

If the lamb is still a little tough, give it 20 mins more until tender. When ready, leave it to rest so it's not piping hot, then serve scattered with pomegranate and herbs, with couscous or rice alongside.

Pea & ham pot pie

Prep:10 mins **Cook:**30 mins

Serves 1

Ingredients

- 100g fresh or frozen soffritto mix (or any ready chopped onions, carrots and celery)
- 2 tsp rapeseed oil
- 2 button mushrooms , quartered
- 2 tbsp frozen peas
- 1 slice of ham , cut into pieces

- 2-3 tbsp cream (of any sort)
- 1 tsp Dijon mustard or other French mustard
- ¼ pack puff pastry (freeze the rest for another time)
- flour (any kind), for rolling

Method

STEP 1

Heat oven to 200C/180C fan/gas 6. Fry the soffrito mix in the oil until it softens and starts to turn golden, add the mushrooms and cook for a couple of mins. Add the peas and ham and cook until the peas are heated through. Stir in the cream and mustard, then turn off the heat. Season well and tip into a pie dish, ovenproof bowl or large shallow mug.

STEP 2

Roll out the pastry using a little of the flour until it is larger than the top of your dish. Lightly score a criss-cross pattern into the pastry. Wet the rim of the dish with water and lift the pastry on top, pressing the pastry on to the edges of the dish.

STEP 3

Cook for 20-25 mins or until the pastry is risen and golden.

One-pan nachos with black beans

Prep:15 mins **Cook:**15 mins

Serves 4-6

Ingredients

- 175g yellow or blue tortilla chips
- 200g fresh tomato salsa
- 150g medium cheddar , grated
- 1 red pepper , quartered, cored and finely chopped
- 400g can black beans , drained
- 1 avocado , diced
- soured cream , to serve

Method

STEP 1

Heat oven to 200C/180C fan/gas 6. Arrange the tortilla chips over two-thirds of the tray, spoon most of the salsa on top and scatter over half of the cheese.

STEP 2

Mix the remaining salsa with the red pepper and beans, and tip onto the empty third of the tray. Scatter over the rest of the cheese. Bake for 10-15 mins or until the cheese has melted. Scatter the avocado over the beans and add dollops of the soured cream to serve.

Layered rainbow salad pots

Prep:25 mins **Cook:**12 mins

Serves 4

Ingredients

- 350g pasta shapes (De Cecco is a good brand that stays nice and firm)
- 200g green beans , trimmed and chopped into short lengths
- 160g can tuna in olive oil, drained
- 4 tbsp mayonnaise

- 4 tbsp natural yogurt
- ½ small pack chives , snipped (optional)
- 200g cherry tomatoes , quartered
- 1 orange pepper , cut into little cubes 195g can sweetcorn, drained

Method

STEP 1

Cook the pasta until it is still a little al dente (2 mins less than the pack instructions) and drain well. Cook the green beans in simmering water for 2 mins, then rinse in cold water and drain well. Mix the tuna with the mayonnaise and yogurt. Add the chives, if using.

STEP 2

Tip the pasta into a large glass bowl or four small ones, or four wide-necked jars (useful for taking on picnics). Spoon the tuna dressing over the top of the pasta. Add a layer of green beans, followed by a layer of cherry tomatoes, then the pepper and sweetcorn. Cover and chill until you're ready to eat.

Slow-cooked Greek lamb

Prep:15 mins **Cook:**5 hrs - 6 hrs

Serves 6

Ingredients

- shoulder of lamb , about 2kg
- 1 garlic bulb , cloves separated but the skin left on
- about 30g anchovies
- 2 tbsp olive oil
- 10 tomatoes , left whole
- 6 carrots , peeled but left whole
- handful fresh sage
- handful fresh rosemary
- handful fresh thyme
- tzatziki , chickpea salad and flatbreads, to serve

Method

STEP 1

Heat oven to 160C/140C fan/gas 3 and sit a shelf as low as possible. Pierce the lamb all over with a small knife, then fill each slit with a garlic clove and half an anchovy fillet. Rub all over with the oil, then season.

STEP 2

Heat a flameproof casserole dish and sear the lamb all over until well browned. Take off the heat, remove the lamb from the dish and tip in the tomatoes, carrots, sage and rosemary. Sit the lamb on top and scatter over the thyme.

STEP 3

Cover the dish, slip it onto the bottom shelf of the oven and cook for 4-5 hrs until pull-apart tender. Carefully lift the lamb from the dish, discard the herbs and roughly squash the tomatoes into the juices. Sit the lamb back in the dish and serve in big shredded chunks with tzatziki, chickpea salad and flatbreads for mopping up the juices.

All-in-one leek & pork pot roast

Prep:15 mins **Cook:**2 hrs

Serves 6

Ingredients

- 1kg boned and rolled shoulder joint of pork
- 6 bay leaves
- 2 garlic cloves , sliced
- bunch of thyme
- 25g butter
- sunflower oil
- 2 onions , peeled and cut into wedges
- 5 juniper berries , crushed
- 1 tsp golden caster sugar

- 1 tbsp white wine vinegar
- 4 whole leeks , trimmed then each cut into 3

- 250ml white wine

Method

STEP 1

Heat oven to 180C/fan 160C/gas 4. I like to untie and unroll the joint then lay 4 bay leaves, the sliced garlic and half the thyme sprigs through it, then retie it. If you're not confident doing this then stab the meat all over and stuff the garlic, bay and thyme into the slits.

STEP 2

Heat the butter and 1 tbsp oil in a casserole, then spend about 10 mins browning the pork on all sides. Add the onions, then continue to cook for about 5 mins until they start to soften. Add the juniper berries, scatter with sugar and add the vinegar. Simmer for a sec, then tuck the leeks and the rest of the bay and thyme in among the pork. Pour over the wine, cover, then cook in the oven for 1½-1¾ hrs until the meat is tender. The dish may now be cooled, then frozen for up to 1 month. Lift the meat from the pan to a board.

STEP 3

Season the veg, then use a slotted spoon to lift it into a bowl. Taste the sauce and, if you think it needs it, reduce to intensify the flavour. Serves slices of meat with a bowl of vegetables and the sauce on the side.

Baked cauliflower pizzaiola

Prep:15 mins **Cook:**40 mins

Serves 4

Ingredients

- 1 large cauliflower, cut into 8 wedges
- 2 tbsp olive oil, plus 1 tbsp for roasting
- 600g ripe tomatoes (we used a mixture of red and yellow cherry tomatoes), halved or quartered depending on their size
- 6 unpeeled garlic cloves, bashed

- small pack basil
- ½ small pack fresh oregano, or 1/2 tsp dried
- pinch of chilli flakes
- 4 tbsp dry white wine

- 2 tbsp grated parmesan, or vegetarian alternative
- 3 tbsp breadcrumbs
- 125g mozzarella (check the pack for a vegetarian brand), torn
- crusty bread, to serve
- green salad, to serve

Method

STEP 1

Heat oven to 200C/180C fan/gas 6. Brush the cauliflower wedges with the 1 tbsp oil, then put them in a large roasting dish. Season and roast for 10 mins or until beginning to soften. Carefully turn the wedges over.

STEP 2

Tuck the tomatoes, garlic and most of the basil and oregano around the cauliflower, then sprinkle with the chilli flakes, wine and 2 tbsp more oil. Season and return to the oven for 25 mins or until the tomatoes are soft and starting to catch here and there. Squish the tomatoes slightly to help the juices flow.

STEP 3

Mix the Parmesan and breadcrumbs together. Tear the mozzarella over the cauliflower and tomatoes, scatter over the cheesy crumbs and bake for 10 mins more or until the topping is crisp and the cauliflower is tender. Top with the rest of the herbs and serve with crusty bread and a green salad.

One-pan coriander-crusted duck, roasted plums & greens

Prep:5 mins **Cook:**15 mins

Serves 2

Ingredients

- 2 tbsp coriander seeds , lightly crushed
- 2 small duck breasts
- 2 plums , stoned, halved and cut into wedges
- 2 pak choi , halved lengthways
- 100ml chicken stock

- 2 tbsp honey
- 1 tbsp soy sauce
- 1 tbsp red wine vinegar
- ¼ tsp chilli flakes , to serve

Method

STEP 1

Heat the oven to 200C/180C fan/gas 6 and put the coriander seeds on a plate. Score the skin of the duck breasts as many times as you can with a small sharp knife, then season with salt and press the skin into the coriander seeds. Heat an ovenproof frying pan and add the breasts, skin-side down. Put a heavy pan on top to weigh them down, and cook for 7-8 mins to render the fat, occasionally draining off the excess.

STEP 2

Add the plums and pak choi to the pan, flip the breasts over and add half the stock. Transfer to the oven and cook for 4-5 mins. Remove the duck breasts from the pan and transfer to a plate to rest along with the pak choi.

STEP 3

Return the pan with the plums to the heat and add the honey, soy, vinegar and remaining stock. Bring to the boil and continue to cook until syrupy. Carve each duck breast into four chunks. Arrange two halves of pak choi over each plate, and nestle the chunks of duck breast and the plums among the greens. Drizzle with the sauce, then sprinkle over the chilli flakes.

Smoky BBQ pork buns with crushed avocado

Prep:5 mins **Cook:**1 hr and 15 mins

Serves 4-6

Ingredients

- 1 tbsp olive or rapeseed oil
- 2 tsp fennel seeds
- 500g pork mince
- 2 tsp sweet paprika
- 2 x 390g cartons passata with onion and garlic
- 100g good-quality barbecue sauce (we used Stokes)
- 400g can pinto or black beans , drained
- 2 ripe avocados
- 1 lime , juiced
- 4-6 rolls or a French stick and grated cheddar, to serve

Method

STEP 1

Heat the oil and fennel in a pan for about 1-2 mins until sizzling. Add the pork and fry until starting to brown in places, breaking it up with your spoon as it cooks. Add the paprika, passata and some seasoning. Cover the pan with a lid and simmer gently for 30 mins, then cook with the lid off for another 15 mins until the mince has broken down and the sauce is thick. Stir through the barbecue sauce and add the beans, then cook for 1 min until warmed through. Turn the heat off but leave on the hob for up to 3 hrs. *Can be chilled for up to two days, or frozen for up to two months. Reheat individual portions in the microwave or in a smaller pan.*

STEP 2

Halve the avocados and scoop the flesh into a bowl. Add the lime juice and some salt. Squash the avocados in your palms through your fingers to make a chunky, crushed guacamole consistency – this is a great job for kids. If you don't want to use your hands, use a fork instead. Cover the surface directly with cling film to prevent it from browning. *Can be chilled in the fridge for up to a day.* Serve the pork mince piled into buns or with a French stick, with the avocado and some grated cheese.

Chicken & mushroom hot-pot

Prep:35 mins **Cook:**25 mins

Serves 4

Ingredients

50g butter or margarine, plus extra for greasing

1 onion, chopped

100g button mushrooms, sliced

40g plain flour

1 chicken stock cube or 500ml fresh chicken stock

pinch of nutmeg

pinch of mustard powder

250g cooked chicken, chopped

2 handfuls of a mixed pack of sweetcorn, peas, broccoli and carrots, or pick your favourites

For the topping

2 large potatoes, sliced into rounds

knob of butter, melted

Method

STEP 1

Heat oven to 200C/180C fan/gas 6. Put the butter in a medium-size saucepan and place over a medium heat. Add the onion and leave to cook for 5 mins, stirring occasionally. Add the mushrooms to the saucepan with the onions.

STEP 2

Once the onion and mushrooms are almost cooked, stir in the flour – this will make a thick paste called a roux. If you are using a stock cube, crumble the cube into the roux now and stir well. Put the roux over a low heat and stir continuously for 2 mins – this will cook the flour and stop the sauce from having a floury taste.

STEP 3

Take the roux off the heat. Slowly add the fresh stock, if using, or pour in 500ml water if you've used a stock cube, stirring all the time. Once all the liquid has been added, season with pepper, a pinch of nutmeg and mustard powder. Put the saucepan back onto a medium heat and slowly bring it to the boil, stirring all the time. Once the sauce has thickened, place on a very low heat. Add the cooked chicken and vegetables to the sauce and stir well. Grease a medium-size ovenproof pie dish with a little butter and pour in the chicken and mushroom filling.

STEP 4

Carefully lay the potatoes on top of the hot-pot filling, overlapping them slightly, almost like a pie top.

STEP 5

Brush the potatoes with a little melted butter and cook in the oven for about 35 mins. The hot-pot is ready once the potatoes are cooked and golden brown.

Easy chicken & chickpea tagine

Prep: 10 mins **Cook:** 1 hr and 15 mins

Serves 4

Ingredients

- 800g skinless boneless chicken thighs , cut into large chunks
- 1 tbsp harissa
- 1 tbsp vegetable oil
- 1 large onion , finely sliced
- 1 tsp ground cinnamon
- 1 tsp ground cumin
- 1 tsp ground turmeric
- 500ml chicken stock
- 400g can chopped tomatoes
- 100g raisins
- 400g can chickpeas , drained and rinsed
- 250g couscous , to serve
- small handful mint , leaves only, to serve

Method

STEP 1

Mix the chicken thighs with the harissa in a large bowl and chill, covered, for 20-30 mins.

STEP 2

Heat the oil in a large flameproof casserole or tagine dish and fry the chicken for 2-3 mins until browned. Remove from the dish and set aside.

STEP 3

Fry the onion for 8-10 mins until soft, then stir in the spices. Return the chicken to the dish, together with the stock, tomatoes and raisins. Season, bring to the boil, then reduce the heat to low. Simmer, covered, for 45 mins.

STEP 4

Add the chickpeas to the dish, and simmer, uncovered, for 15 mins until the sauce reduces slightly and thickens. Serve with couscous and a handful of mint leaves on top.

Berry yogurt pots

Prep:5 mins

Serves 2

Ingredients

- 150g bio yogurt
- 160g blueberries , raspberries or cherries (or a combination)
- 1 tbsp pumpkin seeds , sunflower seeds or flaked almonds
- a little chopped mint (optional)

Method

STEP 1

Spoon the yogurt into two tumblers. Mix the fruit, seeds or nuts of your choice with the mint, if using, and pile into the tumblers.

Chicken, morel mushroom & asparagus one-pan pie

Prep:30 mins **Cook:**35 mins

Serves 5

Ingredients

- 100g fresh morel or 30g dried morels
- 200ml chicken stock (if using fresh morels)
- 50g butter
- 2 shallots , finely sliced
- 3 thyme sprigs , leaves picked
- 2 bay leaves
- 1 tbsp plain flour , plus extra for dusting
- 100ml dry sherry or white wine
- 200ml crème fraîche
- 6 skinless boneless chicken thighs , cut into large chunks
- bunch asparagus , woody ends removed, stalks cut into 4cm pieces
- ½ pack tarragon , leaves roughly chopped, plus a sprig to decorate
- 1 block puff pastry (375g), all-butter is best
- 1 egg , beaten, to glaze

Method

STEP 1

If you are using dried mushrooms, heat the stock and soak them for 10 mins, then remove them, strain the liquid and set it aside. If you're using fresh mushrooms, clean them thoroughly before using. Set a couple of the nicest-looking morels aside to decorate the top of the pie, and halve the rest.

STEP 2

Heat half the butter in a skillet and fry the halved morels for 3-4 mins or until wilted. Scoop them onto a plate and set aside. Heat the remaining butter and gently cook the shallots in the pan with the thyme and bay. Once softened, stir in the flour and cook for 1 min or until you have a sandy paste.

STEP 3

Pour in the sherry and sizzle, then carefully stir in the strained soaking liquid (or 200ml chicken stock if you've used fresh morels), followed by the crème fraîche. Season well and bring the sauce to a gentle simmer. Add the chicken and poach in the sauce for 10 mins or until the chicken is just cooked through. Remove the bay, stir through the asparagus, tarragon and fried morels, then remove from the heat.

STEP 4

Heat oven to 220C/200C fan/gas 8. The pastry needs to sit on top of the ingredients, so if your pan is too deep, use a pie dish instead. Roll out the pastry on a floured surface to the thickness of a £1 coin, then cut the pastry to fit the pan or dish, and drape it over the pie mixture using a rolling pin to help you. Liberally brush with egg, season the pastry with flaky sea salt, and pop your reserved morels on the top. Bake for 20 mins or until the pastry has puffed and is a deep golden brown. Leave tor rest for 5 mins before serving straight from the pan.

One-pan Easter lamb

Prep:20 mins **Cook:**2 hrs and 15 mins

Serves 6

Ingredients

- 1.6kg bone-in leg of lamb
- 50ml olive oil , plus a splash
- 3 oregano sprigs, leaves picked and roughly chopped

- 4 rosemary sprigs, leaves of 2 picked and roughly chopped
- 1 lemon , zested (save the juice for the spring greens, see goes well with)

- 1 garlic bulb , cloves lightly smashed
- 1 red chilli , pierced
- 1kg potatoes , skins on, cut into thick wedges
- 3 fennel bulbs , cut into quarters lengthways, tops removed, green fronds reserved
- 250ml white wine
- 250ml good-quality chicken stock

Method

STEP 1

Take the lamb out of the fridge 1 hr before cooking it and use a sharp knife to make small incisions all over the meat. Mix the oil with the oregano, chopped rosemary and lemon zest. Rub the marinade all over the lamb, massaging it well into the cuts.

STEP 2

Heat oven to 200C/180C fan/gas 6. Put the garlic, chilli, potatoes, fennel and remaining rosemary into a large roasting tin, pour over some olive oil and toss together. Season the lamb generously, then lay it on top of the veg. Roast for 45 mins until the lamb is starting to brown, then pour in the wine and stock. Continue cooking for 30 mins for rare (55C on a cooking thermometer), 35-40 mins for medium rare (60C) or 45 mins for cooked through (70C).

STEP 3

Remove the lamb and rest for up to 30 mins. Turn oven down to 160C/140C fan/gas 3, cover the veg with foil and, while the lamb rests, put back in the oven until braised in the roasting juices. Scatter the fennel fronds over the veg, place the lamb back on top and bring the whole tin to the table to serve.

Coconut fish curry traybake

Prep:15 mins **Cook:**25 mins

Serves 4

Ingredients

- 2 x 250g pouches cooked brown rice
- 160ml can coconut milk
- 4 tbsp Thai red curry paste
- 1 tbsp fish sauce
- 4fillets white fish (around 120g each)
- 200g pack Tenderstem broccoli
- 235g pack pak choi

- ½ small bunch spring onions , sliced on the diagonal
- small pack coriander , leaves picked
- 2 limes , cut into wedges, to serve

Method

STEP 1

Heat oven to 200C/180C fan/gas 6. Tip the rice into a roasting tin. Whisk the coconut milk with the curry paste and fish sauce. Nestle the fish into the rice, put the broccoli, pak choi and half the spring onions on top, and season. Drizzle the coconut mixture over everything, cover with foil and cook in the oven for 25 mins or until the veg is cooked through and the fish is flaking apart.

STEP 2

Serve in bowls, topped with coriander leaves and the remaining spring onions, with lime wedges on the side.

Lemony chicken stew with giant couscous

Prep:25 mins **Cook:**1 hr

Serves 4

Ingredients

- 1 tbsp olive oil
- 2 onions, chopped
- 500g skinless boneless chicken thighs, each cut into 2-3 chunks
- 3 tbsp tagine paste or 2 tbsp ras el hanout
- 2 x 400g cans tomato with chopped mixed olives
- small handful fresh oregano, leaves picked and chopped
- 2 preserved lemons, flesh removed, skin rinsed and finely chopped
- 2 tbsp clear honey
- 1 chicken stock cube
- 200g giant couscous
- handful parsley, chopped

Method

STEP 1

Heat the oil in a large flameproof casserole dish with a lid. Add the onions and cook for 10 mins until starting to caramelise. Push the onions to one side of the dish and add the chicken. Cook over a high heat for 5 mins or so until the chicken is browning.

STEP 2

Add the tagine paste, tomatoes, oregano, preserved lemons and honey, and crumble in the stock cube. Fill one of the tomato cans halfway with water and pour this into the dish. Season with a little salt and plenty of black pepper. Give everything a good stir, then cover with a lid and simmer for 40 mins, on a gentle bubble, or for up to 4 hrs over a very low heat if you're eating at different times.

STEP 3

Add the couscous 10 mins before you're ready to serve, cover and simmer for 10 mins or until cooked. If you're eating at different times, scoop your portion into a pan, add 50g couscous and cook in the same way. Stir in some parsley just before serving.

Smoked chicken, pot barley & cranberry salad

Prep:25 mins **Cook:**20 mins

Serves 4-6

Ingredients

- 200g pot barley , soaked overnight, or pearl barley
- 50g dried cranberries
- 200g green beans , halved
- 1 red-skinned pear
- 1/2 lemon , juiced

For the dressing

- 1½ tbsp cider vinegar
- 3 tsp Dijon mustard
- 1 tbsp maple syrup

- 50g pecans , lightly toasted
- 50g lamb's lettuce
- small bunch of flat-leaf parsley , roughly chopped
- 250g smoked chicken , sliced or torn into chunks

- 4 tbsp extra virgin olive oil
- 4 tbsp hazelnut or walnut oil

Method

STEP 1

Put the soaked pot barley in a pan, cover with water and bring to the boil, or cook the pearl barley following pack instructions. Turn the heat down to a simmer and cook until the barley is tender but retains a little firmness, about 10-15 mins. Drain and leave to cool completely.

Meanwhile, put the cranberries in a small bowl, cover with boiling water and leave to plump up for 20 mins.

STEP 2

Make the dressing by whisking all the ingredients together with a fork. Taste for balance – it should be slightly sweet. Add more vinegar or maple syrup, if you like.

STEP 3

Cook the beans in boiling water for 1-2 mins or until they're tender but still have a little bite. Drain and run cold water over them to help them keep their bright colour. Drain the cranberries and pat them dry with a tea towel. Core, quarter and slice the pear, then toss the slices with the lemon juice.

STEP 4

Put the drained barley, beans, cranberries, pear, pecans, lamb's lettuce, parsley and chicken into a broad, shallow serving bowl with the dressing. Gently toss everything together and serve.

Chicken & new potato traybake

Prep:15 mins **Cook:**1 hr and 15 mins

Serves 2 - 4

Ingredients

- 3 tbsp olive oil
- 500g new potatoes
- 140g large pitted green olives
- 1 lemon, quartered

- 8 fresh bay leaves
- 6 garlic cloves, unpeeled
- 4 large chicken thighs
- bag watercress or salad leaves, to serve

Method

STEP 1

Heat oven to 200C/180C fan/gas 6. Pour the olive oil into a large roasting tin and add the potatoes, olives, lemon quarters, bay leaves and garlic. Toss everything together so it's coated in oil and evenly distributed. Add the chicken thighs, skin-side up, and season.

STEP 2

Put the roasting tin in the oven and roast for 1 hr, basting with the pan juices halfway through cooking. After 1 hr, check that the potatoes are soft and the chicken is cooked through, then return to the oven for a final 15 mins to crisp the chicken skin.

STEP 3

Remove the roasting tin from the oven. Press down on the roasted garlic cloves with the back of a spoon, discard the skins, and mix the mashed garlic with the meat juices. Serve with watercress or your favourite salad leaves on the side.

Red berry granola yogurt pots

Prep:20 mins

Makes 4

Ingredients

- 150g strawberries
- 4 tbsp Greek yogurt

For the coulis

- ½ lemon
- 150g raspberries

For the quick granola

- 1 tbsp coconut oil
- 1 tsp cinnamon
- 150g oats

- 4 tbsp quick granola (see below)

- ½ tbsp honey

- 50g sunflower seeds
- 50g pumpkin seeds
- 2 tbsp honey

Method

STEP 1

To make the coulis, juice the half lemon, then put in a pan with the raspberries and honey. Cook over a gentle heat for a few moments, breaking down with the back of a wooden spoon. Blend to a purée, then push through a sieve and discard the raspberry seeds. Divide between the bottom of four little pots or jars.

STEP 2

To make the quick granola, melt the coconut oil, cinnamon and pinch of salt in a medium pan over a gentle heat. Pour in the oats, seeds and honey and stir well to combine. Continue to move around the pan until evenly browned, about 5 mins. Spread out on a baking sheet to cool.

STEP 3

While it's cooking, slice up the strawberries and divide between the pots, layering up over the coulis. Spoon 1 tbsp of yogurt on top of each pot. Finish each pot with 1 tbsp of granola sprinkled over (the remaining granola will keep in a jar for a week).

One-pan pigs-in-blanket beans

Prep:20 mins **Cook:**40 mins

Serves 8-10

Ingredients

- 1 tbsp sunflower oil
- 6 chipolatas or 12 cocktail sausages
- 200g diced pancetta or bacon lardons
- 2 onions , chopped
- 2 garlic cloves , finely chopped
- 1 tbsp tomato purée

- 75g dark brown soft sugar
- 150ml red wine vinegar
- 2 x 400g cans chopped tomatoes
- 2 x 400g cans cooked white bean , drained
- 6 sage leaves, finely chopped

Method

STEP 1

Heat the oil in a flameproof casserole dish. Sizzle the sausages in the pan until brown on all sides, then lift onto a plate and leave to cool. If you're using chipolatas, cut them into shorter pieces. In the same pan, sizzle the pancetta for 5-8 mins until starting to brown. Scatter the onions over the pancetta and cook until soft, then add the garlic and cook for 1 min longer.

STEP 2

Add the tomato purée and sugar, then pour over the vinegar and chopped tomatoes and use about 100ml of water to rinse out the cans and add that as well. Stir through the beans and sausages, then simmer everything for 20 mins. When the sauce is nice and thick, stir through the sage, simmer for a few minutes more and serve. *The beans can be made up to three days ahead, chilled and reheated.*

One-cup pancakes

Prep:5 mins **Cook:**10 mins

Serves 6

Ingredients

- 1 cup plain flour
- 1½ cups milk
- 1 large egg or 2 medium eggs
- 20g butter

- 2 tbsp vegetable or sunflower oil
- caster sugar and lemon wedges, to serve (optional)

Method

STEP 1

Tip the flour and a pinch of salt into a bowl. Make a well in the centre and pour in the milk and egg. Whisk together, starting in the middle, to create a smooth batter. It should be the thickness of double cream.

STEP 2

Heat a little of the butter and oil in a non-stick frying pan. Add a sixth of the batter to the pan, quickly swirling it so there are no holes. Fry on one side for 1-2 mins then flip over and cook for a further 1 min. Keep on a plate, covered, in a warm oven. Repeat with the remaining batter to make six pancakes in total. Serve with sugar and lemon, if you like.

Brazilian pork stew with corn dumplings

Prep:25 mins **Cook:**2 hrs and 35 mins

Serves 6

Ingredients

- 900g pork shoulder , cut into 4cm chunks
- 2 tbsp sunflower oil
- 2 onions , finely chopped
- 2 celery sticks, finely chopped
- 3 bay leaves

- 1 tbsp oregano leaves (or 2 tsp dried), plus extra, to serve
- 1 tbsp ground cumin
- 1 tbsp ground coriander
- 1 tbsp allspice

- 1 stock cube (beef, pork or chicken)
- 2 x 400g cans chopped tomatoes
- 1 tbsp cocoa powder
- 2 tbsp soft dark brown or muscovado sugar
- 3 tbsp red wine vinegar
- zest and juice 2 oranges
- 2 red chillies , halved lengthways - seeds in or out, depending on whether you like it spicy

For the dumplings

- 100g cold butter , diced
- 200g self-raising flour
- 140g cornmeal or finely ground polenta, plus extra for dusting
- ½ tsp bicarbonate of soda

- bunch spring onions , finely sliced
- 400g sweet potatoes , peeled and cut into 3-4cm/1.25in - 1.5in chunks
- 2 red peppers , deseeded and cut into chunks
- 2 x 400g cans black beans , drained and rinsed

- 140g sweetcorn , from a can, drained, or freshly cut from a cob (just boil for 3 mins first)
- 75ml buttermilk
- 1 medium egg , beaten

Method

STEP 1

Start by getting your biggest flameproof casserole dish and sealing the pork chunks in the oil – they don't have to be very well browned. Do in batches, then transfer to a plate and tip three-quarters of the onions, the celery, bay and oregano into the dish. Add a splash more oil, if you need, and fry gently until softened.

STEP 2

Tip in the spices, stir for 1 min to toast, then return the pork to the dish. Crumble in the stock cube and stir in the tomatoes, cocoa, sugar, 2 tbsp of the vinegar, the zest and juice from 1 orange, and 3 of the chilli halves. Bring to a simmer, then cover and leave to bubble for 1 hr.

STEP 3

Meanwhile, finely chop the reserved chilli half and mix with the remaining onions, the spring onions, and red wine vinegar and the zest and juice from the last orange. Keep cold in the fridge.

STEP 4

After 1 hr, stir the sweet potatoes and red peppers into the stew, then re-cover and simmer for another 30 mins.

STEP 5

When the stew has about 15 mins to go, make the dumplings. Rub the butter into the flour until it resembles fine crumbs, then stir in the cornmeal, bicarb and sweetcorn. Finally, mix in the buttermilk and all but 1 tbsp of the egg to make a soft dough. Season with some salt and roll the mixture into 12 soft dumplings, then roll in a little more cornmeal to coat the tops. Brush the tops with the reserved beaten egg.

STEP 6

Heat oven to 200C/180C fan/gas 6. Stir the beans into the stew, then taste for seasoning. Sit 6 of the dumplings on top of the stew and the rest on a baking tray lined with baking parchment. Put both in the oven – the stew without its lid – and cook for 25 mins until the dumplings are golden and risen.

STEP 7

Carry the stew straight to the table, and sprinkle over a little more oregano before spooning into bowls. Serve the extra dumplings alongside for those who fancy another one, and the onion relish.

Indian chicken protein pots

Prep: 10 mins **Cook:** 1 min

Serves 2

Ingredients

- 90g pack Indian spiced lentils (we used Men's Health from Tesco)
- 160g cherry tomatoes , quartered

- 150g cooked, skinless chicken breast, chopped
- handful fresh coriander , chopped
- 4 tbsp tzatziki

Method

STEP 1

Tear the corner from the lentil pack and microwave on High for 1 min. Leave to cool then tip into 2 large packed lunch pots. Top with the cherry tomatoes and chicken, add the fresh coriander then spoon on the tzatziki. Seal until ready to eat (see tip below).

Chicken biryani

Prep:10 mins **Cook:**30 mins

Serves 4

Ingredients

- 300g basmati rice
- 25g butter
- 1 large onion, finely sliced
- 1 bay leaf
- 3 cardamom pods
- small cinnamon stick
- 1 tsp turmeric
- 4 skinless chicken breasts, cut into large chunks
- 4 tbsp curry paste (we used Patak's balti paste)
- 85g raisins
- 850ml chicken stock
- 30g coriander, ½ chopped, ½ leaves picked and 2 tbsp toasted flaked almonds, to serve

Method

STEP 1

Soak 300g basmati rice in warm water, then wash in cold until the water runs clear.

STEP 2

Heat 25g butter in a saucepan and cook 1 finely sliced large onion with 1 bay leaf, 3 cardamom pods and 1 small cinnamon stick for 10 mins.

STEP 3

Sprinkle in 1 tsp turmeric, then add 4 chicken breasts, cut into large chunks, and 4 tbsp curry paste. Cook until aromatic.

STEP 4

Stir the rice into the pan with 85g raisins, then pour over 850ml chicken stock.

STEP 5

Place a tight-fitting lid on the pan and bring to a hard boil, then lower the heat to a minimum and cook the rice for another 5 mins.

STEP 6

Turn off the heat and leave for 10 mins. Stir well, mixing through 15g chopped coriander. To serve, scatter over the leaves of the remaining 15g coriander and 2 tbsp toasted almonds.

One-pan tikka salmon with jewelled rice

Prep:10 mins **Cook:**45 mins

Serves 3

Ingredients

- 3 tbsp tikka curry paste
- 150ml pot natural low-fat yogurt
- 3 salmon fillets , skinned
- 2 tsp olive oil
- 1 large red onion , chopped

- 1 tsp turmeric
- 50g soft dried apricots , chopped
- 200g brown basmati rice
- 100g pack pomegranate seeds
- small pack coriander , leaves picked

Method

STEP 1

Combine 1 tbsp of the curry paste with 2 tbsp yogurt. Season the salmon and smear the yogurt paste all over the fillets, then set aside.

STEP 2

Heat the oil in a large pan (with a lid) and add the onion. Boil the kettle. Cook the onion for 5 mins to soften, and stir in the remaining curry paste then cook for 1 min more. Add the turmeric, apricots and rice, season well and give everything a good stir. Pour in 800ml water from the kettle. Bring to a boil, and simmer for 15 mins. Cover with a lid, lower the heat to a gentle simmer and cook for 15 mins more.

STEP 3

Uncover the rice and give it a good stir. Put the salmon fillets on top of the rice and re-cover the pan. Turn the heat to its lowest setting and leave undisturbed for 15-20 mins more until the salmon and rice are perfectly cooked. Scatter over the pomegranate seeds and coriander, and serve with the yogurt.

Spicy chicken & bean stew

Prep: 15 mins **Cook:** 1 hr and 20 mins

Serves 6

Ingredients

- 1 ¼kg chicken thighs and drumsticks (approx. weight, we used a 1.23kg mixed pack)
- 1 tbsp olive oil
- 2 onions , sliced
- 1 garlic clove , crushed
- 2 red chillies , deseeded and chopped
- 250g frozen peppers , defrosted
- 400g can chopped tomatoes
- 420g can kidney beans in chilli sauce
- 2 x 400g cans butter beans , drained
- 400ml hot chicken stock
- small bunch coriander , chopped
- 150ml pot soured cream and crusty bread, to serve

Method

STEP 1

Pull the skin off the chicken and discard. Heat the oil in a large casserole dish, brown the chicken all over, then remove with a slotted spoon. Tip in the onions, garlic and chillies, then fry for 5 mins until starting to soften and turn golden.

STEP 2

Add the peppers, tomatoes, beans and hot stock. Put the chicken back on top, half-cover with a pan lid and cook for 50 mins, until the chicken is cooked through and tender.

STEP 3

Stir through the coriander and serve with soured cream and crusty bread.

Chicken & chorizo jambalaya

Prep: 10 mins **Cook:** 45 mins

Serves 4

Ingredients

- 1 tbsp olive oil
- 2 chicken breasts, chopped
- 1 onion, diced
- 1 red pepper, thinly sliced
- 2 garlic cloves, crushed

- 75g chorizo, sliced
- 1 tbsp Cajun seasoning
- 250g long grain rice
- 400g can plum tomato
- 350ml chicken stock

Method

STEP 1

Heat 1 tbsp olive oil in a large frying pan with a lid and brown 2 chopped chicken breasts for 5-8 mins until golden.

STEP 2

Remove and set aside. Tip in the 1 diced onion and cook for 3-4 mins until soft.

STEP 3

Add 1 thinly sliced red pepper, 2 crushed garlic cloves, 75g sliced chorizo and 1 tbsp Cajun seasoning, and cook for 5 mins more.

STEP 4

Stir the chicken back in with 250g long grain rice, add the 400g can of tomatoes and 350ml chicken stock. Cover and simmer for 20-25 mins until the rice is tender.

Summer chicken stew

Prep: 10 mins **Cook:** 55 mins

Serves 4

Ingredients

- 2 tbsp olive oil
- 500g leeks , finely sliced
- 2 plump garlic cloves , finely sliced
- 2 thyme sprigs , leaves picked
- 8 chicken thighs , skinless and boneless
- 500g new potatoes , larger ones quartered, smaller ones halved
- 350ml chicken stock
- 200g green beans
- 350g frozen petit pois
- lemon wedges, to serve

Method

STEP 1

Heat the oil in a large casserole dish over a medium heat. Add the leeks, garlic and thyme, cover and cook gently for 10 mins, stirring occasionally. Season the chicken and tip into the dish with the potatoes.

STEP 2

Turn up the heat, pour in the stock and bring to a simmer. Reduce the heat and allow to gently bubble with the lid on for 35 mins. Add the green beans and peas for the final 10 mins of cooking. Season to taste, then ladle into bowls or lipped plates with a squeeze of lemon.

Moroccan vegetable stew

Prep:30 mins **Cook:**35 mins

Serves 4

Ingredients

- 1 tbsp cold-pressed rapeseed oil
- 1 medium onion , peeled and finely sliced
- 2 thin leeks , trimmed and cut into thick slices
- 2 large garlic cloves , peeled and finely sliced
- 2 tsp ground coriander
- 2 tsp ground cumin
- 1/2 tsp dried chilli flakes
- 1/4 tsp ground cinnamon
- 400g can of chopped tomatoes
- 1 red pepper , deseeded and cut into chunks
- 1 yellow pepper , deseeded and cut into chunks
- 400g can of chickpeas , drained and rinsed
- 100g dried split red lentils
- 375g sweet potatoes , peeled and cut into chunks

- juice 1 large orange plus peel, thickly sliced with a vegetable peeler
- 50g mixed nuts, such as brazils, hazelnuts, pecans and walnuts, toasted and roughly chopped
- 1/2 small pack coriander , roughly chopped, to serve
- full-fat natural bio-yogurt , to serve (optional)

Method

STEP 1

Heat the oil in a large flameproof casserole or saucepan and gently fry the onion and leeks for 10-15 mins until well softened, stirring occasionally. Add the garlic and cook for 2 mins more.

STEP 2

Stir in the ground coriander, cumin, chilli and cinnamon. Cook for 2 mins, stirring occasionally. Season with plenty of ground black pepper. Add the chopped tomatoes, peppers, chickpeas, lentils, sweet potatoes, orange peel and juice, half the nuts and 400ml/14fl oz water and bring to a simmer. Cook for 15 mins, adding a splash of water if the stew looks too dry, and stir occasionally until the potatoes are softened but not breaking apart.

STEP 3

Remove the pan from the heat and ladle the stew into bowls. Scatter with coriander and the remaining nuts and top with yogurt, if using.

Bean & pepper chilli

Prep:15 mins **Cook:**30 mins

Serves 4

Ingredients

- 1 tbsp olive oil
- 1 onion , chopped
- 350g pepper , deseeded and sliced
- 1 tbsp ground cumin
- 1-3 tsp chilli powder , depending on how hot you want your chilli to be
- 1 tbsp sweet smoked paprika
- 400g can kidney bean in chilli sauce
- 400g can mixed bean , drained
- 400g can chopped tomato
- rice , to serve (optional)

Method

STEP 1

Heat the oil in a large pan. Add the onion and peppers, and cook for 8 mins until softened. Tip in the spices and cook for 1 min.

STEP 2

Tip in the beans and tomatoes, bring to the boil and simmer for 15 mins or until the chilli is thickened. Season and serve with rice, if you like.

Greek-style roast chicken

Prep: 10 mins **Cook:** 1 hr

Serves 4

Ingredients

- 750g new potatoes, thickly sliced lengthways
- 2 tbsp olive oil
- 8 chicken thighs, skin on and bone in
- 300g cherry tomatoes

- 100g black olives
- ½ small pack oregano, leaves picked
- 200g pack feta, crumbled into chunks
- 2 tbsp red wine vinegar

Method

STEP 1

Heat oven to 200C/180C fan/gas 6. Put the potatoes in a roasting tin and drizzle with half the oil. Sit the chicken thighs on top, drizzle over the remaining oil and season. Roast in the oven for 30 mins.

STEP 2

Add the cherry tomatoes, olives, oregano leaves and feta, then drizzle with the red wine vinegar. Return to the oven for another 25-30 mins until the chicken is cooked through and golden.

Spicy harissa chicken with lentils

Prep: 10 mins **Cook:** 45 mins

Serves 4

Ingredients

- 1 tbsp olive oil
- 1 red onion , chopped
- 1 garlic clove , crushed
- 50g harissa
- 500g chicken thigh , skin removed, boned and diced
- 1 medium carrot , grated
- 200g dried puy lentils
- 2 x 400g cans chopped tomatoes
- 1.2l stock , made from 1 chicken or vegetable stock cube
- flat-leaf parsley , to serve (optional)

Method

STEP 1

Heat the oil in a large frying pan. Fry the onion on a low heat for 5-6 mins until softened and translucent. Add the garlic and cook for 1 min more.

STEP 2

Stir in the harissa, add the chicken and cook until well browned all over. Stir in the carrot, lentils and tomatoes, then add the stock so the chicken is fully immersed.

STEP 3

Reduce the heat and cook, uncovered, for 30-35 mins until the chicken is thoroughly cooked, and the lentils are tender and have absorbed the liquid. Season well, scatter with parsley (if using) and serve.

Andalusian-style chicken

Prep: 10 mins **Cook:** 25 mins - 30 mins

Serves 4 as part of a tapas spread

Ingredients

- large pinch of saffron

- ½ chicken stock cube , crumbled into 100ml boiling water
- 2 tbsp olive oil
- 1 small onion , thinly sliced
- 2 large chicken breasts or 6 boneless, skinless thighs, cut into bite-sized pieces
- large pinch of ground cinnamon
- 1 red chilli , deseeded and chopped
- 2 tbsp sherry vinegar
- 1 tbsp clear honey
- 6 cherry tomatoes , quartered
- 1 tbsp raisins
- handful of coriander , roughly chopped
- 25g toasted pine nuts or almonds
- crusty bread , to serve

Method

STEP 1

Add the saffron to the hot stock to soak. Heat the oil in a medium pan and cook the onion until it is soft and just beginning to turn golden. Push to the side of the pan and add the chicken. Cook for a few mins until the chicken is browned all over.

STEP 2

Add the cinnamon and chilli, and cook for a couple of mins. Add the stock, vinegar, honey, tomatoes and raisins. Bring to the boil, turn down the heat and simmer for 10 mins until the sauce is reduced and the chicken is cooked through. When ready to serve, scatter with the coriander and nuts, and serve with bread on the side.

Spicy asparagus & chorizo baked egg

Prep:5 mins **Cook:**20 mins

Serves 1

Ingredients

- 125g asparagus , cut into 3cm pieces
- 20g diced chorizo
- ½ tsp hot smoked paprika
- 75g frozen spinach
- 1 tbsp half-fat crème fraîche
- 1 large egg
- flatbread , to serve (optional)

Method

STEP 1

Heat a small non-stick frying pan over a medium heat, add the asparagus and chorizo and fry for 8 mins. Stir through the paprika, cooking for a further 1 min.

STEP 2

Stir the spinach into the pan and cook for 5 mins until wilted before stirring through the crème fraîche. Season, then make a well in the middle of the mixture and crack the egg into it. Cover the pan and cook for 5-6 mins or until the egg is just set. Serve with a flatbread, if you like.

Winter berry & white chocolate pots

Prep:40 mins **Cook:**30 mins

plus 8 hrs chilling

Serves 6

Ingredients

- pomegranate seeds , to serve

For the white chocolate layer

- 100ml double cream
- 200g white chocolate , chopped
- 2 large lemons , zested

For the berry layer

- 300g mixed frozen berries , defrosted
- 150g frozen raspberries
- 2 tbsp lemon juice
- 600ml double cream
- 160g golden caster sugar

For the pistachio shortbread

- 100g unsalted butter , softened
- 50g golden caster sugar
- 135g plain flour
- 50g pistachios , finely chopped, plus extra to serve

Method

STEP 1

For the white chocolate layer, heat the cream in a saucepan until steaming and bubbles appear around the edge. Add the chocolate and lemon zest and stir until melted. Set six short tumblers tilted on their sides in a muffin tin (this is how you get a slanted layer). Pour the mixture into the glasses, then chill for 4 hrs, or until set.

STEP 2

For the berry layer, put all the frozen berries in a food processor and whizz until puréed. Push through a sieve using a wooden spoon directly into a jug, then stir through the lemon juice. Put the cream and sugar in a saucepan and warm gently until the sugar melts. Increase the heat and boil for 3 mins, stirring continuously. Remove from the heat and stir through the purée. Cool for 15 mins before sitting the glasses upright and pouring over the white chocolate layer. Chill for 4 hrs or until set.

STEP 3

Heat the oven to 170C/150C fan/gas 3. Line a baking sheet with non-stick parchment. To make the shortbread, put the butter and sugar in a bowl and beat with an electric whisk until pale and fluffy. Mix in ¼ tsp fine sea salt, the flour and pistachios to get a stiff dough, then bring together with your hands into a smooth ball. Put between two sheets of baking parchment and roll out to around ½cm. Chill for 20 mins. Cut into 20 rounds about 4cm and place on the baking sheet. Bake for 20-25 mins, then slide off the sheet onto a wire rack and leave to cool. *Can be made two days ahead and kept in an airtight container.*

STEP 4

When ready to serve, top the possets with the chopped pistachios and pomegranate seeds, and serve with the pistachio biscuits.

Jambalaya

Prep:20 mins **Cook:**50 mins

Serves 4 - 6

Ingredients

- 2 tbsp olive oil
- 6 skinless boneless chicken thighs fillets, chopped
- 200g cooking chorizo , sliced
- 2 onions , finely sliced
- 4 garlic cloves , crushed
- 2 red peppers , sliced
- 2 celery sticks , chopped
- 1 tsp fresh thyme leaves
- 1 tsp dried oregano

- ½ tsp garlic salt
- 1 tsp smoked paprika
- 1 tsp cayenne pepper
- ½ tsp mustard powder
- pinch of white pepper
- 300g long-grain rice
- 400g can cherry tomatoes

- 300ml chicken stock
- 12 large raw tiger prawns (whole in their shells)
- 12 mussels , cleaned and de-bearded
- 24 clams
- ½ small pack parsley , chopped
- 4 spring onions , sliced on a diagonal

Method

STEP 1

Heat oven to 200C/180C fan/ gas 6. Heat the oil in a heavy-based flameproof casserole dish on a medium-high heat. Season the chicken thighs, add to the dish and cook for 4 mins until they start to brown, stirring occasionally so they don't stick. Add the chorizo and cook for a further 4 mins until it releases its oils and has started to crisp. Remove the meat with a slotted spoon and set aside on a plate.

STEP 2

Add the onions to the chorizo oils, lower the heat and soften for 8 mins. Stir through the garlic, peppers, celery, thyme and oregano , and cook for 2 mins more.

STEP 3

Return the meat to the dish, add the garlic salt, paprika, cayenne, mustard powder and white pepper, and cook for 2 mins until fragrant. Stir in the rice, then the tomatoes. Add the stock and give it all a really good stir. Bring to the boil , then cover with a well-fitting lid and put in the oven for 20 mins.

STEP 4

Take from the oven and fluff up the rice with a big fork. Fold through the prawns, then put the mussels and clams on top. Put the lid on ,return to the oven for 10 mins, then take the dish out and give everything a good stir. Sprinkle with the parsley and spring onions to serve.

Tuna Niçoise protein pot

Prep:10 mins **Cook:**10 mins

Serves 1

Ingredients

- 1 large egg
- 80g green beans
- 1 tomato , amber or red, quartered

- 120g can tuna in spring water
- 1½ -2 tbsp French dressing

Method

STEP 1

Boil the egg for 8-10 mins depending on if you want a soft or hard yolk, then at the same time steam the green beans for 6 mins above the pan until tender. Cool the egg and beans under running water then carefully shell and quarter the egg. Leave to cool.

STEP 2

Tip the beans into a large packed lunch pot. Top with the tomato, tuna and quartered egg and spoon on the French dressing. Seal until ready to eat (see tip below).

Pesto chicken stew with cheesy dumplings

Prep:50 mins **Cook:**2 hrs and 20 mins

Serves 8

Ingredients

- 2 tbsp olive oil
- 12-15 chicken thighs , skin removed, bone in
- 200g smoked bacon lardon or chopped bacon
- 1 large onion , chopped
- 4 celery sticks, chopped
- 3 leeks , chopped

- 4 tbsp plain flour
- 200ml white wine
- 1l chicken stock
- 2 bay leaves
- 200g frozen pea
- 140g sundried tomato
- 140g fresh pesto
- small bunch basil , chopped

For the dumplings

- 140g butter
- 250g self-raising flour

- 100g parmesan , grated
- 50g pine nut

Method

STEP 1

Heat the oil in a large casserole dish. Brown the chicken until golden on all sides – you might have to do this in batches – remove the chicken from the pan as you go and set aside.

STEP 2

Add the lardons to the pan and sizzle for a few mins, then add the onion, celery and leeks, and cook over a medium heat for 8-10 mins until the vegetables have softened. Stir in the flour, season and cook for a further 2 mins.

STEP 3

Gradually stir in the wine and allow it to bubble away, then stir in the stock. Return the chicken to the pan with the bay leaves and cover with a lid. Reduce the heat and simmer gently for 1½ hrs or until the chicken is tender. The stew can now be cooled and frozen if you're making ahead. Just defrost thoroughly, then gently warm through back in the pan before continuing.

STEP 4

Heat oven to 200C/180C fan/gas 6. Add the peas, sundried tomatoes, pesto and basil to the stew. To make the dumplings, rub the butter into the flour until it resembles fine breadcrumbs. Mix in the grated cheese and add 150ml water, mixing with a cutlery knife to bring the crumbs together to form a light and sticky dough. Break off walnut-sized lumps and shape into small balls. Roll the tops of the dumplings in the pine nuts so a few stick to the outside, then place the dumplings on top of the stew and scatter with any remaining nuts. Put the dish in the oven and bake for 25 mins until the dumplings are golden brown and cooked through. Serve with mashed potato and extra veg if you like.

Pesto chicken stew with cheesy dumplings

Prep:50 mins **Cook:**2 hrs and 20 mins

Serves 8

Ingredients

- 2 tbsp olive oil
- 12-15 chicken thighs , skin removed, bone in
- 200g smoked bacon lardon or chopped bacon
- 1 large onion , chopped
- 4 celery sticks, chopped
- 3 leeks , chopped

- 4 tbsp plain flour
- 200ml white wine
- 1l chicken stock
- 2 bay leaves
- 200g frozen pea
- 140g sundried tomato
- 140g fresh pesto
- small bunch basil , chopped

For the dumplings

- 140g butter
- 250g self-raising flour

- 100g parmesan , grated
- 50g pine nut

Method

STEP 1

Heat the oil in a large casserole dish. Brown the chicken until golden on all sides – you might have to do this in batches – remove the chicken from the pan as you go and set aside.

STEP 2

Add the lardons to the pan and sizzle for a few mins, then add the onion, celery and leeks, and cook over a medium heat for 8-10 mins until the vegetables have softened. Stir in the flour, season and cook for a further 2 mins.

STEP 3

Gradually stir in the wine and allow it to bubble away, then stir in the stock. Return the chicken to the pan with the bay leaves and cover with a lid. Reduce the heat and simmer gently for 1½ hrs or until the chicken is tender. The stew can now be cooled and frozen if you're making ahead. Just defrost thoroughly, then gently warm through back in the pan before continuing.

STEP 4

Heat oven to 200C/180C fan/gas 6. Add the peas, sundried tomatoes, pesto and basil to the stew. To make the dumplings, rub the butter into the flour until it resembles fine breadcrumbs. Mix in the grated cheese and add 150ml water, mixing with a cutlery knife to bring the crumbs together to form a light and sticky dough. Break off walnut-sized lumps and shape into small balls. Roll the tops of the dumplings in the pine nuts so a few stick to the outside, then place the dumplings on top of the stew and scatter with any remaining nuts. Put the dish in the oven and bake for 25 mins until the dumplings are golden brown and cooked through. Serve with mashed potato and extra veg if you like.

Salted caramel popcorn pots

Prep:10 mins **Cook:**15 mins

plus at least 8 hrs chilling

Serves 2

Ingredients

- 400ml double cream
- 200ml milk
- 140g toffee popcorn , plus a little to serve
- 2 gelatine leaves
- 4 tbsp caramel from a can (we used Carnation)
- ¼-½ tsp flaky sea salt

Method

STEP 1

Pour the cream and milk into a large pan, add the popcorn and bring to a gentle simmer, pushing the popcorn under the liquid and squashing gently on the bottom of the pan. Bubble for 1 min, then remove from the heat, transfer to a jug and chill for at least 6 hrs, or preferably overnight.

STEP 2

Strain the popcorn cream back into a clean pan and gently reheat, discarding the remaining bits of popcorn. Meanwhile, place the gelatine leaves in cold water to soften for 3-5 mins. When the popcorn cream is steaming and the gelatine is soft, remove it from the water and squeeze out any excess drops. Place in the hot popcorn cream and stir until dissolved. Set aside to cool a little.

STEP 3

Mix the caramel with the sea salt – start with 1/4 tsp, taste, then add more if you think it needs it. Divide the salted caramel between 2 glasses or pots. Pour the popcorn cream on top and chill for at least 2 hrs, or overnight.

STEP 4

Serve each pot topped with a few pieces of toffee popcorn and dive in!

Sticky orange chicken with parsnips, maple & pecans

Prep: 25 mins **Cook:** 1 hr and 5 mins

Serves 2

Ingredients

- 2 blood oranges , 1 juiced, 1 thickly sliced
- 3 tbsp maple syrup
- 2 tbsp olive oil
- 2 tbsp sherry vinegar
- 1 tbsp wholegrain mustard
- 1 tbsp cranberry or redcurrant jelly , melted
- 2 parsnips , quartered, peeled and the core cut out and discarded

- 4 chicken thighs , skin on
- 140g small shallots , left whole but peeled
- 2 thyme sprigs , broken up a bit
- 25g pecans , barely chopped
- mixed leaf salad or wilted spinach, to serve (optional)
- cooked rice , to serve (optional)

Method

STEP 1

Heat oven to 180C/160C fan/gas 4. Juice 1 of the oranges and whisk together with the maple syrup, olive oil, vinegar, mustard and cranberry jelly. Cut the parsnips into chunky lengths. Put the parnips, chicken thighs and shallots in a roasting tin – make sure everything can sit in a single layer but quite snug. Drizzle over half the orange sauce with some seasoning and toss to coat everything. Roast for 35 mins.

STEP 2

Remove the tin from the oven and poke the orange slices in among everything. Scatter over the thyme and drizzle over the rest of the orange sauce. Roast for another 15 mins until the chicken is tender and cooked through, and everything is sticky and golden. Mix in the pecans and cook for another 5 mins. Serve straight away, remembering to scrape out all the sticky juices from the tin, and eat with a mixed leaf salad or some wilted spinach, plus a little rice to soak up the sauce, if you like.

Chorizo & cabbage stew

Prep: 10 mins **Cook:** 20 mins

Serves 2

Ingredients

- 100g piece of spicy chorizo sausage (not cooking chorizo), halved lengthways and shredded
- 1 onion , halved and thinly sliced
- 100g baby Charlotte potatoes , thinly sliced
- 400g can chopped tomatoes
- 1 chicken stock cube
- 100g Savoy cabbage , shredded

Method

STEP 1

Put the chorizo, onion and potatoes in a large non-stick pan. Leave to fry in the oil that comes from the chorizo, stirring occasionally for about 5 mins.

STEP 2

Tip in the tomatoes with 2 cans of water, add the stock cube, then bring to the boil. Cover and simmer for 10 mins. Add the cabbage, then cover and cook 3-5 mins more until it is just tender. Ladle into bowls and serve.

Chicken casserole with herby dumplings

Prep: 30 mins **Cook:** 1 hr and 10 mins

Serves 6

Ingredients

- 12 skinless chicken pieces - a mixture of thighs and drumsticks on the bone, and halved chicken breasts
- 3 tbsp plain flour
- 2 tbsp sunflower oil
- 2 onions, sliced
- 2 carrots, diced
- 200g bacon lardons, smoked or unsmoked, or streaky rashers, snipped
- 3 bay leaves
- 3 sprigs thyme
- 250ml red wine

- 3 tbsp tomato paste
- 1 chicken stock cube

For the herby dumplings

- 140g cold butter, diced
- 250g self-raising flour
- 2 tbsp chopped mixed herb - try parsley, thyme and sage or chives

Method

STEP 1

Heat oven to 180C/160C fan/gas 4. Toss the chicken pieces with the flour and some salt and pepper, to coat them – it's easy to do this in a plastic food bag.

STEP 2

Heat the oil in a casserole with a lid. Brown the chicken pieces well on all sides – you'll need to do this in batches. Remove all the pieces to a plate, and tip the onions, carrot, lardons, bay and thyme into the pan. Cook gently for 10 mins until the onion is softened.

STEP 3

Return the chicken pieces, with any juices that have collected on the plate. Then pour in the red wine, 250ml water and tomato paste and crumble in the stock cube. Add a splash more of water if you need, until the chicken is almost covered. Bring to the boil, then cover with a lid and bake in the oven for 20 mins. Remove the lid and bake for another 10 mins while you make the dumplings.

STEP 4

Rub the butter into the flour with your fingertips until it feels like fine breadcrumbs. Stir in the herbs with ½ tsp salt and some pepper. Drizzle over 150ml water, and stir in quickly with a cutlery knife to form a light dough. Use floured hands to shape into ping pong sized balls.

STEP 5

Place the dumplings on top of the stew and bake for 20 mins more until the dumplings are cooked through.

One-pan lentil dhal with curried fish & crispy skin

Prep:20 mins **Cook:**1 hr

Serves 2

Ingredients

- 2 onions , chopped
- 1 tbsp grated ginger
- 1 tbsp sunflower oil , plus a splash
- 2 tbsp mild curry powder , plus 1/2 tsp
- 1 tsp brown mustard seeds
- 1 ½ tsp onion or nigella seeds
- 85g red lentils
- 85g split peas or chana dhal lentils
- 1 ¼ tsp ground turmeric
- 400g can coconut milk
- 3 tbsp natural yogurt , plus extra for serving
- 2 firm white fish fillets with skin - we used sustainably sourced cod
- 2 plum tomatoes , diced
- juice 1 lime , plus 1 cut into wedges, to serve
- handful coriander leaves
- 2 tbsp crispy onions from a tub
- warm naan , to serve
- mango chutney , to serve

Method

STEP 1

Heat oven to 200C/180C fan/gas 6. Mix the onions, ginger, oil, 2 tbsp curry powder, the mustard seeds and 1 tsp of the onion or nigella seeds with 5 tbsp water in a baking dish roughly 25 x 18cm. Roast in the oven for 10-15 mins until the onions are softened.

STEP 2

Stir in the lentils, split peas or chana dhal lentils, 1 tsp of the turmeric, the coconut milk and half a can of water, and return to the oven for 30 mins. Meanwhile, mix together the remaining turmeric, onion seeds and curry powder and the yogurt. Carefully slice the skin off the fish fillets and place on kitchen paper to dry, then rub the yogurt all over the fish fillets and leave to marinate in the fridge while you cook the lentils.

STEP 3

Give the dhal a good stir, mix in the tomatoes and juice from 1 lime, plus1 tsp salt. Sit the fish fillets on top witha sprinkling of extra seasoning. Return to the oven and cook for a further 15 mins until the fish is done. Removethe dish from the oven and turnon the grill. Place the fish skin ona baking tray, sprinkle with some salt and grill, turning, until crispy. Snap into pieces and scatter over the fish with some coriander and the crispy onions. Serve with more yogurt, lime wedges, naan bread and mango chutney.

146

Muffin tin chilli pots

Prep:15 mins **Cook:**5 mins

Serves 2

Ingredients

- 400g can kidney beans in spicy sauce
- 4 medium tortilla wraps
- 400g can chopped tomatoes with herbs
- 230g green salad

Method

STEP 1

Heat oven to 200C/180C fan/gas 6. Simmer the beans and tomatoes in a pan for 15 mins, then season.

STEP 2

Meanwhile, grease four holes of a muffin tin with oil. Line each with a tortilla, making a cup, and fill with a ball of foil. Bake for 5 mins until lightly crisped. Remove the foil, divide the bean mix between the tortilla cups and serve with the green salad.

5-minute mocha pots

Prep:5 mins **Cook:**2 mins

Serves 4

Ingredients

- 200g milk or dark chocolate with coffee, broken into chunks
- 300ml pot double cream
- 1 tsp vanilla extract
- 2 tbsp crème fraîche

Method

STEP 1

Melt the chocolate in the microwave for 2 mins, stirring halfway through, or over a pan of gently simmering water. Leave to cool a little.

STEP 2

Using an electric whisk, whip the double cream with the vanilla in a bowl until lightly whipped. Fold in the cooled, melted chocolate until fully combined.

STEP 3

Split the mixture between four small bowls or ramekins and serve topped with a dollop of crème fraîche. If you aren't serving straight away, chill in the fridge and then add the crème fraîche just before bringing to the table.

One-pan pigeon breast with spinach & bacon

Prep:5 mins **Cook:**15 mins

Serves 2

Ingredients

- 50g butter
- 100g smoked bacon lardons or chopped smoked bacon
- 2 slices white sourdough

- 2 pigeon breasts
- 50g chestnut or wild mushrooms , sliced
- 200g spinach
- 1 tbsp red wine or sherry vinegar

Method

STEP 1

Heat half the butter in a large frying pan, then fry the bacon for 5 mins until starting to crisp. Transfer to a plate using a slotted spoon. Fry the bread in any leftover bacon fat for 1 min on each side until crisp and golden, then transfer to a plate and set aside.

STEP 2

Season the pigeon generously with salt and pepper, and heat the remaining butter in the pan until sizzling. Sear the pigeon for 2-3 mins on each side until golden, then transfer to a chopping board and leave to rest.

STEP 3

Return the fried bacon to the pan and turn up the heat. Scatter over the mushrooms and fry for 3-4 mins until softened, then add the spinach, season and splash in the vinegar. Turn the heat up to high and stir-fry until the spinach is wilted. Divide the spinach mixture between the fried bread slices. Finely slice the pigeon breasts, arrange over the spinach and serve.

Moroccan fish stew

Prep: 15 mins **Cook:** 35 mins

Serves 4

Ingredients

- 1 tbsp cold-pressed rapeseed oil
- 1 medium onion , thinly sliced
- 2 thin leeks , trimmed and sliced
- 1/2 small fennel bulb , quartered and very thinly sliced
- 2 large garlic cloves , finely sliced
- 2 tsp ground coriander
- 1 tsp ground cumin
- 1/2 tsp chilli flakes
- 1/4 tsp ground cinnamon
- 400g can chopped tomatoes
- 375g sweet potatoes , peeled and cut into chunks
- 1 yellow pepper , deseeded and cut into chunks
- 1 red pepper , deseeded and cut into chunks
- 400g can chickpeas , drained and rinsed
- juice 1 large orange , the peel thickly sliced with a vegetable peeler
- 200g skinless line-caught cod , haddock or pollock fillet, cut into chunks
- 200g skinless wild salmon , cut into chunks
- 1/2 small pack flat-leaf parsley , roughly chopped

Method

STEP 1

Heat the oil in a large flameproof casserole dish or saucepan and gently fry the onion, leeks and fennel for 10 mins, stirring occasionally, or until the veg is well softened and lightly browned. Add the garlic and spices, and cook for 30 secs more. Season well with ground black pepper.

STEP 2

Tip in the chopped tomatoes, sweet potatoes, peppers, chickpeas, orange juice and peel with 300ml water and bring to a gentle simmer. Cover loosely and cook for 20 mins, stirring occasionally, until the potatoes are softened but not breaking apart.

STEP 3

Add the fish pieces on top of the bubbling liquid and cover. Poach over a medium heat for 3-4 mins or until the fish is just cooked. Adjust the seasoning and serve scattered with parsley.

Mexican beef chilli

Prep:15 mins **Cook:**2 hrs and 15 mins

Serves 15

Ingredients

- up to 6 tbsp sunflower oil
- 4kg stewing beef
- 4 white onions , sliced
- 4 tbsp chipotle paste
- 8 garlic cloves , crushed
- 50g ginger , grated
- 1 tbsp ground cumin
- 2 tsp ground cinnamon
- 1 tbsp plain flour
- 2l beef stock
- 3 x 400g cans chopped tomatoes
- 1 tbsp dried oregano
- 5 x 400g cans pinto or kidney beans , drained

Method

STEP 1

Heat a small drizzle of the oil in an extra-large flameproof dish. Brown the meat in batches, adding a drop more oil, remove from the dish and set aside. Add 1 tbsp oil to the dish, then the onions, and cook for 7-10 mins or until caramelised.

STEP 2

Stir the chipotle paste, garlic, ginger, cumin, cinnamon and flour in with the onions and cook for a couple of mins. Gradually add the stock, stirring all the time, so it's fully mixed in with the other ingredients. Add the tomatoes and oregano, season and simmer for 10 mins.

STEP 3

Now tip in the beef, cover and simmer very gently for about 1 hr 45 mins until tender, removing the lid and adding the beans for the final 15 mins. If the sauce is thin, let it boil down for a further 5-10 mins with the lid off. Before serving, adjust the seasoning. Serve with the garlic bread and salsa.

Bean & barley soup

Prep:5 mins **Cook:**1 hr

Serves 4

Ingredients

- 2 tbsp vegetable oil
- 1 large onion , finely chopped
- 1 fennel bulb , quartered, cored and sliced
- 5 garlic cloves , crushed
- 400g can chickpea , drained and rinsed
- 2 x 400g cans chopped tomatoes

- 600ml vegetable stock
- 250g pearl barley
- 215g can butter beans , drained and rinsed
- 100g pack baby spinach leaves
- grated parmesan , to serve

Method

STEP 1

Heat the oil in a saucepan over a medium heat, add the onion, fennel and garlic, and cook until softened and just beginning to brown, about 10-12 mins.

STEP 2

Mash half the chickpeas and add to the pan with the tomatoes, stock and barley. Top up with a can of water and bring to the boil, then reduce the heat and simmer, covered, for 45 mins or until the barley is tender. Add another can of water if the liquid has significantly reduced.

STEP 3

Add the remaining chickpeas and the butter beans to the soup. After a few mins, stir in the spinach and cook until wilted, about 1 min. Season and serve scattered with Parmesan.

Beef in red wine with melting onions

Prep:20 mins **Cook:**2 hrs and 10 mins

Serves 4 - 6

Ingredients

- 25g butter
- 2 large onions, sliced into rings
- 6 garlic cloves, halved
- 3 tbsp plain flour
- 600g piece beef skirt or slices of shin, cut into large chunks
- 2 tbsp olive or rapeseed oil
- 3 bay leaves
- 400ml red wine
- 1 tbsp tomato purée
- 300ml strong beef stock
- 250g mushrooms, halved (we used small Portobello mushrooms)
- chopped parsley, to serve (optional)

Method

STEP 1

Heat oven to 150C/130C fan/gas 2. In a large, heavy-based flameproof casserole dish with a lid, melt the butter over a medium heat. Add the onions and garlic, cook for 10 mins until starting to brown, then transfer to a small plate.

STEP 2

Put the flour in a large plastic food bag with plenty of black pepper. Add half the beef, shake to coat, then remove, leaving some flour in the bag. Add the rest of the beef and shake to coat in the remaining flour.

STEP 3

Heat the oil in the same casserole dish you cooked the onions in (there's no need to clean it first). Add the beef and bay leaves, and fry until the meat is browned all over. Pour in the wine and return the onions to the dish. Add the tomato purée and stock, stir and return to a simmer. Cover with the lid and put in the oven to stew for 1 hr.

STEP 4

After 1 hr, add the mushrooms and return to the oven for another hour. Taste the meat – if it's tender, remove from the oven. If it's still a little firm, cook for 30 mins more and test again. Serve scattered with parsley, if you like.

Chilli Marrakech

Prep:30 mins Cook 1 hr (plus heating from frozen)

Serves 10

Ingredients

- 1 ½ tbsp cumin seed
- 1 tbsp olive oil
- 3 onions , halved and thinly sliced
- 3 x 400g packs lean lamb mince
- 2 tbsp finely chopped ginger
- 4 garlic cloves , finely chopped
- 2 x 400g cans chopped tomatoes
- 1 tbsp paprika
- 1 tbsp ground cinnamon
- 1 ½ tbsp ground coriander
- 3 tbsp harissa
- 3 red peppers , deseeded and cut into large chunks
- 2 x 400g cans chickpeas , drained
- 2 x 20g packs coriander , most chopped, a few leaves left whole to serve
- 500ml beef or lamb stock , made with 2 cubes

Method

STEP 1

Heat your largest non-stick wok or pan, tip in the cumin seeds and toast for a few secs. Remove. Add the oil to the pan and fry the onions for 5 mins until starting to colour. Add the mince, ginger and garlic, and cook, breaking up the mince with your wooden spoon, until no longer pink. Drain any excess liquid or fat from the pan.

STEP 2

Stir in the tomatoes, toasted cumin, remaining spices and harissa – add more spice if you like an extra kick. Add the peppers, chickpeas, three-quarters of the chopped coriander and the stock. Cover and cook for 40 mins, stirring occasionally, until the sauce is slightly thickened. Remove from the heat. Cool, then stir in the remaining chopped coriander. Can be served or frozen at this point.

STEP 3

Pack into freezer bags and smooth the mince through the bag to flatten. Use within 3 months. To serve, remove from the bags and heat from frozen in a pan on the hob with a little water until bubbling hot, then scatter with coriander.

Lamb & aubergine pastitsio

Prep:20 mins **Cook:**1 hr and 50 mins

Serves 6

Ingredients

- 1 tbsp olive oil
- 2 onions , chopped
- 3 garlic cloves
- 300g frozen lamb mince
- 2 tsp cinnamon
- ½ tsp ground allspice
- 1 tbsp dried oregano or mixed herbs
- 1 large aubergine , cut into small cubes
- 1 lamb or beef stock cube
- 2 x 400g cans chopped tomatoes
- 400g macaroni
- For the bechamel sauce
- 1l semi-skimmed milk
- 2 bay leaves
- 85g butter
- 85g plain flour
- 75g parmesan , plus extra for the top

Method

STEP 1

Heat the oil in a large pan. Add the onions and cook until softened, then add the garlic and stir around the pan for 1 min more. Scoop the onions to one side of the pan, add the lamb and cook until browned. Pour off any excess oil from the pan.

STEP 2

Add the spices and oregano, then tip in the aubergine. Fry for another 5 mins until the aubergine has softened a little, then crumble in the stock cube and add the tomatoes, along with half a can of water. Season, cover the pan and simmer for 30 mins.

STEP 3

Uncover the lamb mince and continue to simmer until the sauce is thick and clinging to the meat – about 15 mins. Meanwhile, make the béchamel sauce. Warm the milk in a large pan with the bay leaves. Melt the butter in another large pan, stir in the flour to make a paste, then add the warm milk, ladle by ladle, stirring well between each addition, until you have a thick, smooth sauce. Season well and add the Parmesan. Meanwhile, cook the pasta following pack instructions, then drain.

STEP 4

Heat oven to 200C/180C fan/gas 6. Tip the mince into a large baking dish. Mix the macaroni into the cheesy sauce and pour this over the lamb. Sprinkle with the remaining cheese. Can now be frozen, defrost before cooking. Bake for 35-40 mins until golden brown and crispy on top. Leave to cool for 5 mins before serving.

Keralan chicken coconut ishtu

Prep: 20 mins **Cook:** 1 hr and 20 mins

Serves 4

Ingredients

- 5 tbsp coconut oil or vegetable oil
- 5cm/2in cinnamon stick
- 6 green cardamom pods
- 4 cloves
- 10 black peppercorns , lightly crushed
- 1 star anise
- 15 curry leaves
- 1 medium onion , finely sliced
- thumb-sized piece of ginger , peeled and finely chopped
- 6 garlic cloves , finely chopped
- 2-3 green chillies
- 2 tsp fennel seeds
- ½ tsp ground turmeric
- 1 tbsp ground coriander
- 600g chicken thighs , skinned
- handful green beans , ends trimmed, halved if very long
- 400ml can coconut milk
- 2 tbsp coconut cream
- 1 tsp vinegar (or to taste)
- large handful baby spinach , blanched and water squeezed out
- small handful fresh coriander , to garnish

Method

STEP 1

Heat the oil in a wide pan (a karahi or wok is ideal), then add the cinnamon stick, cardamom pods, cloves, peppercorns and star anise. Once the seeds have stopped popping, add the curry leaves and the onion and cook over a medium heat until translucent. Add the ginger, garlic and green chillies, and sauté gently for 1-2 mins or until the garlic is cooked.

STEP 2

Grind the fennel seeds to a fine powder in a spice grinder or with a pestle and mortar, then add to the pan with the turmeric, ground coriander and a pinch of salt. Add a splash of water and cook for 2 mins. Put the chicken in the pan and cook in the spice paste for 2 mins. Add water to come a third of the way up the chicken, bring to a boil, then reduce the heat and cook, covered, for 1 hr, stirring occasionally.

STEP 3

Once the liquid has reduced, add the green beans and coconut milk (including the thin milk that collects at the bottom of the can), cover and cook for another 10 mins. Uncover and cook off most of the excess liquid, stirring occasionally. Check the chicken is cooked all the way through. Stir in the coconut cream, vinegar and spinach, and bring to a simmer. Taste and adjust the seasoning, and serve topped with the coriander.

Spiced lamb pilaf

Prep: 10 mins **Cook:** 40 mins

Serves 6

Ingredients

- 2 tbsp vegetable oil
- 1 large onion , finely chopped
- 3 garlic cloves , finely chopped
- 4 cloves
- 8 cardamom pods , crushed
- 2 tsp turmeric
- 1 large cinnamon stick
- 2 lamb stock cubes
- 450g basmati rice
- 500g lamb leftovers, shredded

- 100g raisins
- 5 spring onions , finely sliced
- 3 tomatoes , deseeded and roughly chopped
- small bunch parsley , roughly chopped, plus a few leaves picked, to serve
- small bunch coriander , roughly chopped, plus a few leaves picked, to serve
- 50g flaked almonds , toasted
- 200ml natural yogurt , to serve

Method

STEP 1

Put the oil in a large pan over a medium heat. Add the onion to the pan and cook until soft and translucent, about 15 mins. Add the garlic and spices, and stir in for 2 mins.

STEP 2

Crumble the stock cubes into 1.2 litres of just-boiled water. Add the rice and shredded lamb to the pan. Stir well to coat the grains in the oil and spices, then pour over the stock. Bring to the boil, then cover with a lid and lower the heat. Cook for 12 mins or until the rice is tender and the stock absorbed.

STEP 3

Once the rice is ready, remove from the heat and add the raisins, spring onions, tomatoes and herbs, mixing well. Season to taste and serve topped with more herbs, almonds and a drizzle of natural yogurt.

Steak & broccoli protein pots

Prep:10 mins **Cook:**9 mins

Serves 2

Ingredients

- 250g pack wholegrain rice mix with seaweed (Merchant Gourmet)
- 2 tbsp chopped sushi ginger
- 4 spring onions , the green part finely chopped, the white halved lengthways and cut into lengths
- 160g broccoli florets, cut into bite-sized pieces
- 225g lean fat-trimmed fillet steak

Method

STEP 1

Tip the rice mix into a bowl and stir in the ginger, chopped onion greens and 4 tbsp water. Add the broccoli and the spring onion whites, but keep the onions together, on top, as you will need them in the next step. Cover with cling film, pierce with the tip of a knife and microwave for 5 mins.

STEP 2

Meanwhile heat a non-stick frying pan and sear the steak for 2 mins each side, then set aside. Take the onion whites from the bowl and add to the pan so they char a little in the meat juices while the steak rests.

STEP 3

Tip the rice mixture into 2 large packed lunch pots. Slice the steak, pile the charred onions on top and seal until you're ready to eat (see tip below).

Lemon drizzle cake

Prep: 15 mins **Cook:** 45 mins

Cuts into 10 slices

Ingredients

- 225g unsalted butter, softened
- 225g caster sugar
- 4 eggs
- 225g self-raising flour
- 1 lemon, zested
- For the drizzle topping
- 1½ lemons, juiced
- 85g caster sugar

Method

STEP 1

Heat the oven to 180C/160C fan/gas 4.

STEP 2

Beat together the butter and caster sugar until pale and creamy, then add the eggs, one at a time, slowly mixing through.

STEP 3

Sift in the self-raising flour, then add the lemon zest and mix until well combined.

STEP 4

Line a loaf tin (8 x 21cm) with greaseproof paper, then spoon in the mixture and level the top with a spoon.

STEP 5

Bake for 45-50 mins until a thin skewer inserted into the centre of the cake comes out clean.

STEP 6

While the cake is cooling in its tin, mix together the lemons juice and caster sugar to make the drizzle.

STEP 7

Prick the warm cake all over with a skewer or fork, then pour over the drizzle – the juice will sink in and the sugar will form a lovely, crisp topping.

STEP 8

Leave in the tin until completely cool, then remove and serve. *Will keep in an airtight container for 3-4 days, or freeze for up to 1 month.*

Roast dinner for one

Prep:10 mins **Cook:**35 mins

Serves 1

Ingredients

- 2 tbsp olive oil
- 1 large chicken breast , skin on
- 6 small new potatoes (about 200g/7oz), halved
- 2 carrots , cut into rounds
- 1 small onion , cut into wedges
- 3 broccoli spears or florets
- 3 thyme sprigs
- 1 bay leaf
- 150ml chicken stock , warmed
- ½ tbsp plain flour

Method

STEP 1

Heat oven to 200C/180C fan/gas 6. Rub 1 tbsp of the oil over the chicken skin,then season. Put the potatoes, carrots, onion and broccoli in a small roasting tin with the thyme and bay leaf. Drizzle over the remaining oil, season well and toss together to coat everything. Sit the chicken breast on top and roast in the oven for 25-30 mins until it is cooked and the veg are tender.

STEP 2

Remove the chicken, potatoes and broccoli from the roasting tin and set aside while you make the gravy. Set the tin on the hob over a high heat and add the stock. Bring to the boil, then simmer for a few mins. Add the plain flour and stir constantly to remove any lumps. Once the sauce has thickened, take off the heat.

STEP 3

Slice the chicken breast into 3-4 pieces at an angle. Serve with the potatoes, broccoli, carrots and onion gravy.

Spaghetti puttanesca

Prep: 15 mins **Cook:** 20 mins

Serves 4

Ingredients

- 3 tbsp olive oil
- 1 onion, finely chopped
- 2 large garlic cloves, crushed
- ½ tsp chilli flakes (optional)
- 400g can chopped tomatoes
- 5 anchovy fillets, finely chopped
- 120g pitted black olives
- 2 tbsp capers, drained
- 300g dried spaghetti
- ½ small bunch of parsley, finely chopped

Method

STEP 1

Heat the oil in a non-stick pan over a medium-low heat. Add the onion along with a generous pinch of salt and fry for 10 mins, or until soft. Add the garlic and chilli, if using, and cook for a further minute.

STEP 2

Stir the tomatoes, anchovies, olives and capers into the onion, bring to a gentle simmer and cook, uncovered, for 15 mins. Season to taste.

STEP 3

Meanwhile, bring a large pan of salted water to the boil. Cook the spaghetti following pack instructions, then drain and toss with the sauce and parsley.

Slow-braised pork shoulder with cider & parsnips

Prep: 20 mins **Cook:** 2 hrs and 30 mins

Serves 5

Ingredients

- 2 tbsp olive oil
- 1kg/2lb 4oz pork shoulder , diced
- 2 onions , sliced
- 2 celery sticks, roughly chopped
- 3 parsnips , cut into chunks
- 2 bay leaves

- 1 tbsp plain flour
- 330ml bottle cider
- 850ml chicken stock
- handful parsley , chopped
- mashed potato and greens , to serve (optional)

Method

STEP 1

Heat oven to 180C/160C fan/gas 4. Heat the oil in a large lidded flameproof casserole and brown the meat in batches, then set aside. Fry the onions, celery and parsnips with the bay leaves for 10 mins until golden brown. Sprinkle in the flour and give a good stir, then add the pork and any juices back to the dish.

STEP 2

Add the cider and stock so that the meat and vegetables are covered. Season and bring to a simmer, then cover and put in the oven for 2 hrs. Serve sprinkled with parsley, with mashed potato and greens, if you like.

Thai shellfish pot

Prep: 30 mins **Cook:** 20 mins

Serves 4

Ingredients

- 1 tbsp sunflower oil
- 4 lime leaves
- 200g prepared squid , cut into rings

- 400ml coconut milk
- 300g boneless firm white fish like monkfish or hake, cut into chunks

- 500g mussels , cleaned

For the curry paste

- 1 large shallot , sliced
- 1 lemongrass stalk , shredded
- 2 red chillies , sliced
- 5 garlic cloves
- thumb-sized piece of galangal or ginger, peeled and sliced

- 1 tsp ground coriander
- 1 tsp ground cumin
- 2 tbsp fish sauce
- 4 tbsp roasted peanuts
- 1 tsp soft brown sugar

To serve

- chopped coriander
- sliced chillies

- lime wedges

Method

STEP 1

For the curry paste, put all the ingredients in a spice grinder or blender and blitz to a fine paste. Will keep in the fridge for a few days.

STEP 2

Heat the oil in a wok or casserole dish. Add the curry paste and lime leaves, and fry for a minute or so. Stir in the squid so it's coated all over in the paste, then pour over the coconut milk. Bring to a simmer, then submerge the white fish in the sauce and scatter over the mussels. Cover the wok with a lid and cook for
5-8 mins or until the mussel shells are fully open and the fish is just cooked. Sprinkle with the coriander and chilli, then put in the middle of the table, along with the lime wedges. Let everyone help themselves.

Steak & broccoli protein pots

Prep:10 mins **Cook:**9 mins

Serves 2

Ingredients

- 250g pack wholegrain rice mix with seaweed (Merchant Gourmet)

- 2 tbsp chopped sushi ginger

- 4 spring onions , the green part finely chopped, the white halved lengthways and cut into lengths
- 160g broccoli florets, cut into bite-sized pieces
- 225g lean fat-trimmed fillet steak

Method

STEP 1

Tip the rice mix into a bowl and stir in the ginger, chopped onion greens and 4 tbsp water. Add the broccoli and the spring onion whites, but keep the onions together, on top, as you will need them in the next step. Cover with cling film, pierce with the tip of a knife and microwave for 5 mins.

STEP 2

Meanwhile heat a non-stick frying pan and sear the steak for 2 mins each side, then set aside. Take the onion whites from the bowl and add to the pan so they char a little in the meat juices while the steak rests.

STEP 3

Tip the rice mixture into 2 large packed lunch pots. Slice the steak, pile the charred onions on top and seal until you're ready to eat (see tip below).

Roast dinner for one

Prep:10 mins **Cook:**35 mins

Serves 1

Ingredients

- 2 tbsp olive oil
- 1 large chicken breast , skin on
- 6 small new potatoes (about 200g/7oz), halved
- 2 carrots , cut into rounds
- 1 small onion , cut into wedges
- 3 broccoli spears or florets
- 3 thyme sprigs
- 1 bay leaf
- 150ml chicken stock , warmed
- ½ tbsp plain flour

Method

STEP 1

Heat oven to 200C/180C fan/gas 6. Rub 1 tbsp of the oil over the chicken skin,then season. Put the potatoes, carrots, onion and broccoli in a small roasting tin with the thyme and bay leaf. Drizzle over the remaining oil, season well and toss together to coat everything. Sit the chicken breast on top and roast in the oven for 25-30 mins until it is cooked and the veg are tender.

STEP 2

Remove the chicken, potatoes and broccoli from the roasting tin and set aside while you make the gravy. Set the tin on the hob over a high heat and add the stock. Bring to the boil, then simmer for a few mins. Add the plain flour and stir constantly to remove any lumps. Once the sauce has thickened, take off the heat.

STEP 3

Slice the chicken breast into 3-4 pieces at an angle. Serve with the potatoes, broccoli, carrots and onion gravy.

Rosemary chicken with oven-roasted ratatouille

Prep:15 mins **Cook:**40 mins

Serves 4

Ingredients

- 1 aubergine , cut into chunky pieces
- 2 courgettes , sliced into half-moons
- 3 mixed peppers , deseeded and roughly chopped
- 2 tsp finely chopped rosemary , plus 4 small sprigs

- 2 large garlic cloves , crushed
- 3 tbsp olive oil
- 4 skinless, boneless chicken breasts
- 250g cherry or baby plum tomato , halved

Method

STEP 1

Heat oven to 200C/180C fan/gas 6. In a large roasting tin, toss together the aubergine, courgettes and peppers with half the chopped rosemary, half the garlic, 2 tbsp oil and some seasoning. Spread out the vegetables in an even layer, then roast in the oven for 20 mins.

STEP 2

Meanwhile, mix remaining rosemary, garlic and oil together. Slash each of the chicken breasts 4-5 times with a sharp knife, brush over the flavoured oil, season and chill for 15 mins.

STEP 3

After veg have cooked for 20 mins, stir in the tomatoes. Make spaces in the roasting tin and nestle the chicken breasts amongst the vegetables. Place a rosemary sprig on top of each chicken breast. Return the tin to the oven for 18-20 mins, until the chicken is cooked through and the vegetables are lightly caramelised. Serve with some new potatoes, if you like.

Honey, mustard & crème fraîche baked chicken

Prep:10 mins **Cook:**45 mins

Serves 4

Ingredients

- 4 tbsp crème fraîche
- 2 tbsp grainy mustard
- 2 garlic cloves , crushed
- 150ml chicken stock
- 8 skin-on chicken drumsticks and thighs
- 500g baby potatoes
- 200g green beans
- 2 tbsp clear honey
- ½ small bunch tarragon , roughly chopped

Method

STEP 1

Heat oven to 200C/180C fan/gas 6. Mix together the crème fraîche, mustard, garlic and stock with some seasoning. Arrange the chicken, skin-side up, in a roasting tray just large enough for the chicken and vegetables.

STEP 2

Tuck the potatoes and beans in between the chicken pieces. Pour over the stock mixture then season the chicken and drizzle with honey. Cook for 40-45 mins until the chicken is cooked through and the potatoes tender. Scatter over the tarragon before serving

Pork & chorizo enchiladas

Prep:30 mins **Cook:**1 hr and 10 mins

Serves 8

Ingredients

- 1 tbsp olive oil
- 2 large onions , halved and thinly sliced
- 3 garlic cloves , chopped
- 1 tbsp ground cumin
- 2 heaped tbsp smoked paprika
- 2 tsp cinnamon
- 2 red chillies , halved, deseeded and sliced
- 500g pack pork mince
- 2 x 200g packs cooking chorizo sausages, removed from their skins

- 680g bottle passata
- 1 pork or chicken stock cube
- 2 red and 2 green peppers , deseeded, quartered and sliced
- 2 x 400g cans borlotti beans , drained
- 30g pack coriander , chopped
- 500g tub fromage frais (not fat-free)
- 1 large egg
- 2 packs of 8 soft corn tortillas
- 140g mature cheddar , grated
- green salad , to serve

Method

STEP 1

Heat the oil in a large, deep pan and fry the onions and garlic for about 10 mins. Add the spices and half the chilli, and cook for 1 min more. Tip in the pork and chorizo, turn up the heat and fry the meat, stirring and breaking it down until it changes colour. Pour in the passata and 300ml water, then crumble in the stock cube. Pile in the peppers, stir, cover and simmer over a low heat for 30 mins until the meat and peppers are tender. Stir in the beans and two-thirds of the coriander.

STEP 2

Meanwhile, tip the fromage frais (with any liquid in the tub) into a bowl, and beat in the egg, remaining coriander and seasoning. Get out 2 ovenproof and freezer-proof dishes.

STEP 3

Spoon the meat onto the centre of the tortillas, roll up and arrange 8 in each dish. Spoon half of the fromage frais mixture on top and smooth it to cover the tortillas. Scatter each with half the cheese and remaining chillies. If eating now, heat oven to 190C/170C fan/gas 5 and bake for 25 mins until golden, then serve. If freezing, when cold cover with cling film and foil. Will keep for 3 months. To serve, thaw in the fridge and reheat uncovered as above, adding an extra 15 mins to the time, checking that it is hot all the way through. You can also bake from frozen. Put the dish (covered with fresh foil) on a baking tray in the oven, then heat oven to 180C/160C fan/gas 4 and bake for 2 hrs. Don't put the frozen dish in a preheated oven as it might crack – it's better to let it heat slowly. Remove the foil and bake for 20 mins more. Serve with a green salad.

Chicken & egg-fried rice

Prep:5 mins **Cook:**10 mins

Serves 4

Ingredients

- 1 tbsp sunflower oil
- 3 eggs, beaten with some seasoning
- 320g pack mixed stir-fry vegetable
- 1 tbsp mild curry powder
- 140g frozen sweetcorn
- 600g cooked rice see tip, below
- 1 roasted chicken breast, finely shredded
- 2 tbsp low-salt soy sauce
- 2 tbsp sweet chilli sauce
- 2 tbsp ketchup

Method

STEP 1

Heat a splash of oil in a large frying pan and tip in the beaten eggs. Swirl the pan to coat in a thin layer of egg and cook for a few mins until set. Tip onto a chopping board, roll up, slice thinly and set aside.

STEP 2

Heat a little more oil, add the stir-fry veg, curry powder and sweetcorn with a splash of water. Cook for 1-2 mins until the veg starts to wilt, then tip into a bowl. Add the last of the oil to the pan, tip in the rice and chicken, mix well, then add the soy sauce, sweet chilli, ketchup, a splash of water and some black pepper.

STEP 3

Finally, add the eggs and the veg, toss together and heat through until hot. Tip into bowls and serve immediately.

Sausages with oregano, mushrooms & olives

Prep: 10 mins **Cook:** 20 mins

Serves 4

Ingredients

- 450g pack reduced-fat sausage
- 1 tsp sunflower oil
- 2 tsp dried oregano
- 2 garlic cloves , sliced
- 400g can chopped or cherry tomato
- 200ml beef stock
- 100g pitted black olives in brine
- 500g pack mushroom , thickly sliced

Method

STEP 1

Using kitchen scissors, snip the sausages into meatball-size pieces. Heat a large pan and fry the pieces in the oil for about 5 mins until golden all over.

STEP 2

Add the oregano and garlic, fry for 1 min more, then tip in the tomatoes, stock, olives and mushrooms.

STEP 3

Simmer for 15 mins until the sausages are cooked through and the sauce has reduced a little. Serve with mashed potato or pasta.

Vegetarian casserole

Prep: 10 mins **Cook:** 40 mins

Serves 4

Ingredients

- 1 tbsp olive or rapeseed oil
- 1 onion, finely chopped
- 3 garlic cloves, sliced
- 1 tsp smoked paprika
- ½ tsp ground cumin
- 1 tbsp dried thyme
- 3 medium carrots, sliced (about 200g)

- 2 medium sticks celery, finely sliced (about 120g)
- 1 red pepper, chopped
- 1 yellow pepper, chopped
- 2 x 400g cans tomatoes or peeled cherry tomatoes
- 1 vegetable stock cube made up to 250ml (we used 1 Knorr vegetable stock pot)
- 2 courgettes, sliced thickly (about 300g)
- 2 sprigs fresh thyme
- 250g cooked lentils (we used Merchant Gourmet ready-to-eat Puy lentils)

Method

STEP 1

Heat 1 tbsp olive or rapeseed oil in a large, heavy-based pan. Add 1 finely chopped onion and cook gently for 5 – 10 mins until softened.

STEP 2

Add 3 sliced garlic cloves, 1 tsp smoked paprika, ½ tsp ground cumin, 1 tbsp dried thyme, 3 sliced carrots, 2 finely sliced celery sticks, 1 chopped red pepper and 1 chopped yellow pepper and cook for 5 minutes.

STEP 3

Add two 400g cans tomatoes, 250ml vegetable stock (made with 1 stock pot), 2 thickly sliced courgettes and 2 sprigs fresh thyme and cook for 20 - 25 minutes.

STEP 4

Take out the thyme sprigs. Stir in 250g cooked lentils and bring back to a simmer. Serve with wild and white basmati rice, mash or quinoa.

Thai shellfish pot

Prep:30 mins **Cook:**20 mins

Serves 4

Ingredients

- 1 tbsp sunflower oil
- 4 lime leaves
- 200g prepared squid , cut into rings
- 400ml coconut milk
- 300g boneless firm white fish like monkfish or hake, cut into chunks
- 500g mussels , cleaned

For the curry paste

- 1 large shallot , sliced
- 1 lemongrass stalk , shredded
- 2 red chillies , sliced
- 5 garlic cloves
- thumb-sized piece of galangal or ginger, peeled and sliced

- 1 tsp ground coriander
- 1 tsp ground cumin
- 2 tbsp fish sauce
- 4 tbsp roasted peanuts
- 1 tsp soft brown sugar

To serve

- chopped coriander
- sliced chillies

- lime wedges

Method

STEP 1

For the curry paste, put all the ingredients in a spice grinder or blender and blitz to a fine paste. Will keep in the fridge for a few days.

STEP 2

Heat the oil in a wok or casserole dish. Add the curry paste and lime leaves, and fry for a minute or so. Stir in the squid so it's coated all over in the paste, then pour over the coconut milk. Bring to a simmer, then submerge the white fish in the sauce and scatter over the mussels. Cover the wok with a lid and cook for
5-8 mins or until the mussel shells are fully open and the fish is just cooked. Sprinkle with the coriander and chilli, then put in the middle of the table, along with the lime wedges. Let everyone help themselves.

Seafood paella

Prep:40 mins **Cook:**1 hr and 10 mins

Serves 8

Ingredients

- 20-24 raw shell-on king prawns
- 2 tbsp olive oil
- 500g monkfish, cut into chunks

- 1 large onion, finely chopped
- 500g paella rice
- 4 garlic cloves, sliced

- 2 tsp smoked paprika
- 1 tsp cayenne pepper (optional)
- pinch of saffron
- ½ x 400g can chopped tomatoes (save the rest for the stock, below)

- 500g mussels, cleaned
- 100g frozen peas
- 100g frozen baby broad beans
- handful parsley leaves, roughly chopped

For the stock

- 1 tbsp olive oil
- 1 onion, roughly chopped
- ½ x 400g can chopped tomatoes

- 6 garlic cloves, roughly chopped
- 1 chicken stock cube
- 1 star anise

Method

STEP 1

Peel and de-vein the prawns, reserving the heads and shells. Return the prawns to the fridge.

STEP 2

To make the stock, heat the oil in a large pan over a medium-high heat and add the onion, tomatoes, garlic, and reserved prawn shells and heads. Cook for 3-4 mins, then pour in 2 litres of water and add the stock cube and star anise. Bring to a boil, then simmer for 30 mins. Leave to cool slightly, then whizz in batches in a blender or food processor. Strain through a fine sieve.

STEP 3

Heat the oil in a large paella pan or an extra-large frying pan. Brown the monkfish for a few mins each side, then remove and set aside. Add the onion and fry for 4-5 mins until softened.

STEP 4

Stir in the rice and cook for 30 secs to toast. Add the garlic, paprika, cayenne (if using) and saffron, cook for another 30 secs, then stir in the tomatoes and 1.5 litres of the fish stock. Bring to the boil, then turn down to a simmer and cook, stirring, for about 10 mins (the rice should still be al dente). Return the monkfish to the pan with the prawns, mussels, peas and broad beans.

STEP 5

Cover the pan with a large baking tray, or foil, and cook on a low heat for another 10-15 mins until the mussels are open and the prawns are cooked through. Scatter over the parsley before serving.

Oven-baked leek & bacon risotto

Prep:10 mins **Cook:**30 mins

Serves 4

Ingredients

- 1 tbsp olive oil
- 6 rashers smoked back bacon, roughly chopped
- 2 leeks, halved lengthways and finely sliced
- 250g risotto rice
- 700ml hot chicken or vegetable stock
- 175g frozen peas
- 3 tbsp soft cheese
- zest 1 lemon

Method

STEP 1

Heat oven to 200C/180C fan/ gas 6. Tip the oil into an ovenproof casserole dish. Add bacon and fry for 2 mins. Add the leeks and cook until soft, but not coloured, for about 4-5 mins. Tip in rice and cook for 1 min more. Pour over stock. Cover and place in the oven for 20 mins, stirring halfway.

STEP 2

When rice is just tender and all liquid is absorbed, remove from oven and stir in peas. Place back in oven for 2 mins more. Remove and stir in cheese. Add zest and season.

Chicken, ginger & green bean hotpot

Prep:10 mins **Cook:**25 mins

Serves 2

Ingredients

- ½ tbsp vegetable oil
- 2cm piece ginger , cut into matchsticks
- 1 garlic clove , chopped
- ½ onion , thinly sliced into half moons
- 1 tbsp fish sauce
- ½ tbsp soft brown sugar
- 250g skinless chicken thigh fillets, trimmed of all fat and cut in half
- 125ml chicken stock

- 50g green bean , trimmed and cut into 2.5cm lengths
- 1 tbsp chopped coriander
- steamed rice , to serve

Method

STEP 1

Heat the oil in a saucepan over a medium-high heat. Add the ginger, garlic and onion, and stir-fry for about 5 mins or until lightly golden. Add the fish sauce, sugar, chicken and stock. Cover and cook over a medium heat for 15 mins.

STEP 2

For the final 3 mins of cooking, add the green beans. Remove from the heat and stir through half of the coriander. Serve with steamed rice and the remaining coriander scattered over.

Baked eggs with potatoes, mushrooms & cheese

Prep:10 mins **Cook:**25 mins

Serves 4

Ingredients

- 3 baking potatoes , peeled and cubed
- 1 tbsp sunflower oil
- 600g mushrooms , quartered
- 2 garlic cloves , sliced
- 2 tbsp thyme leaves
- 140g cheddar , grated
- 4 eggs

Method

STEP 1

Heat oven to 200C/180C fan/gas 6. Put the potatoes in a pan of water, bring to the boil, cook for 5 mins, then drain. Heat the oil in a large frying pan. Cook the potatoes, mushrooms and garlic for 5-8 mins to soften the mushrooms and brown the edges of the potatoes. Stir in half the thyme and cook for 1 min more.

STEP 2

Spoon the potato mixture into a baking dish and sprinkle with the cheese and the remaining thyme. Make holes in the mixture and break in 4 eggs. Bake in the oven for 12-15 mins until the eggs are set and the cheese has melted.

One-pan summer eggs

Prep:5 mins **Cook:**12 mins

Serves 2

Ingredients

- 1 tbsp olive oil
- 400g courgettes (about 2 large ones), chopped into small chunks
- 200g/7oz pack cherry tomatoes , halved

- 1 garlic clove , crushed
- 2 eggs
- few basil leaves , to serve

Method

STEP 1

Heat the oil in a non-stick frying pan, then add the courgettes. Fry for 5 mins, stirring every so often until they start to soften, add the tomatoes and garlic, then cook for a few mins more. Stir in a little seasoning, then make two gaps in the mix and crack in the eggs. Cover the pan with a lid or a sheet of foil, then cook for 2-3 mins until the eggs are done to your liking. Scatter over a few basil leaves and serve with crusty bread.

Pot-roast beef with French onion gravy

Prep:15 mins **Cook:**2 hrs and 15 mins

Serves 4

Ingredients

- 1kg silverside or topside of beef with no added fat
- 2 tbsp olive oil
- 8 young carrots, tops trimmed (but leave a little, if you like)
- 1 celery stick, finely chopped
- 200ml white wine
- 600ml rich beef stock

- 2 bay leaves
- 500g onion
- a few thyme sprigs
- 1 tsp butter
- 1 tsp light brown or light muscovado sugar
- 2 tsp plain flour

Method

STEP 1

Heat oven to 160C/140C fan/gas 3. Rub the meat with 1 tsp of the oil and plenty of seasoning. Heat a large flameproof casserole dish and brown the meat all over for about 10 mins. Meanwhile, add 2 tsp oil to a frying pan and fry the carrots and celery for 10 mins until turning golden.

STEP 2

Lift the beef onto a plate, splash the wine into the hot casserole and boil for 2 mins. Pour in the stock, return the beef, then tuck in the carrots, celery and bay leaves, trying not to submerge the carrots too much. Cover and cook in the oven for 2 hrs. (I like to turn the beef halfway through cooking.)

STEP 3

Meanwhile, thinly slice the onions. Heat 1 tbsp oil in a pan and stir in the onions, thyme and some seasoning. Cover and cook gently for 20 mins until the onions are softened but not coloured. Remove the lid, turn up the heat, add the butter and sugar, then let the onions caramelise to a dark golden brown, stirring often. Remove the thyme sprigs, then set aside.

STEP 4

When the beef is ready, it will be tender and easy to pull apart at the edges. Remove it from the casserole and snip off the strings. Reheat the onion pan, stir in the flour and cook for 1 min. Whisk the floury onions into the beefy juices in the casserole, to make a thick onion gravy. Taste for seasoning. Add the beef and carrots back to the casserole, or slice the beef and bring to the table on a platter, with the carrots to the side and the gravy spooned over.

Korean rice pot

Prep:15 mins **Cook:**20 mins

Serves 4

Ingredients

- 500ml/ 18 fl oz hot chicken stock
- 250g/ 9oz long grain rice
- 300g/ 11oz cooked turkey , diced
- 250g/ 9oz baby spinach
- 2 carrots , shredded
- 1 tsp toasted sesame oil
- 1 tsp toasted sesame seed
- 2 tbsp vegetable oil

- 4 eggs
- 2 tbsp thick chilli sauce

Method

STEP 1

Pour the chicken stock into a large pan and bring to the boil. Add the rice and turkey, bring back to the boil and simmer for 12-15 mins until the stock has been absorbed and rice is tender.

STEP 2

Meanwhile, put the spinach in a colander and pour over a kettle of hot water to lightly wilt. Keep the spinach and carrots separate, but dress both with the sesame oil and seeds.

STEP 3

Cover the cooked rice with a lid and leave to sit for a couple of mins. Meanwhile, heat vegetable oil in a non-stick pan set over a high heat. Fry eggs so the white crisps up nicely round the edges.

STEP 4

Spoon the rice into large bowls and arrange the spinach and carrots on top. Finish each with a fried egg and a dollop of chilli sauce. Serve immediately.

Greek lamb with orzo

Prep:20 mins **Cook:**2 hrs and 35 mins

Serves 6

Ingredients

- 1kg shoulder of lamb
- 2 onions, sliced
- 1 tbsp chopped oregano, or 1 tsp dried
- ½ tsp ground cinnamon
- 2 cinnamon sticks, broken in half
- 2 tbsp olive oil
- 400g can chopped tomato
- 1.2l hot low-sodium chicken or vegetable stock
- 400g orzo (see know-how below)
- freshly grated parmesan, to serve

Method

STEP 1

Heat oven to 180C/fan 160C/gas 4. Cut the lamb into 4cm chunks, then spread over the base of a large, wide casserole dish. Add the onions, oregano, cinnamon sticks, ground cinnamon and olive oil, then stir well. Bake, uncovered, for 45 mins, stirring halfway.

STEP 2

Pour over the chopped tomatoes and stock, cover tightly, then return to the oven for 1½ hrs, until the lamb is very tender.

STEP 3

Remove the cinnamon sticks, then stir in the orzo. Cover again, then cook for a further 20 mins, stirring halfway through. The orzo should be cooked and the sauce thickened. Sprinkle with grated Parmesan and serve with crusty bread.

Poached salt beef & root veg

Prep: 20 mins **Cook:** 3 hrs

Serves 8

Ingredients

- 1 ½l chicken stock
- 4 tbsp English mustard
- 8 baby heritage carrots , peeled
- 8 baby turnips , peeled and halved
- 16 medium salad potatoes , scrubbed
- 1 ½kg piece salt beef
- 16 French Breakfast radishes , tops left on
- 16 cocktail or small pickled onions
- small handful picked dill fronds

Method

STEP 1

Heat oven to 160C/140C fan/gas 3. Pour the stock into a flameproof roasting tin or shallow casserole dish, add 3 tbsp mustard and bring to the boil. Turn off the heat, then scatter in all of the vegetables except the radishes and onions. Nestle the beef in the middle, fat-side up. Brush the top of the beef with the remaining mustard, scatter over 1 tsp cracked black pepper, cover with a lid or foil and put in the oven for to braise for 3 hrs, or until the beef is tender.

STEP 2

Leave everything to cool a little, then lift the meat from the dish, transfer to a board and carve into thin slices. Stir the onions through the broth with the other vegetables, then divide the braised vegetables between bowls and pour in the mustardy cooking juices. Drape the slices of beef over the top, then poke in some radishes so they're in amongst it all. Scatter the dill over just before serving.

Turkish one-pan eggs & peppers (Menemen)

Prep: 10 mins **Cook:** 25 mins

Serves 4

Ingredients

- 2 tbsp olive oil
- 2 onions , sliced
- 1 red or green pepper , halved deseeded and sliced
- 1-2 red chillies , deseeded and sliced
- 400g can chopped tomatoes
- 1-2 tsp caster sugar
- 4 eggs
- small bunch parsley , roughly chopped
- 6 tbsp thick, creamy yogurt
- 2 garlic cloves , crushed

Method

STEP 1

Heat the oil in a heavy-based frying pan. Stir in the onions, pepper and chillies. Cook until they begin to soften. Add the tomatoes and sugar, mixing well. Cook until the liquid has reduced, season.

STEP 2

Using a wooden spoon, create 4 pockets in the tomato mixture and crack the eggs into them. Cover the pan and cook the eggs over a low heat until just set.

STEP 3

Beat the yogurt with the garlic and season. Sprinkle the menemen with parsley and serve from the frying pan with a dollop of the garlic-flavoured yogurt.

Chipotle bean chilli with baked eggs

Prep: 5 mins **Cook:** 30 mins

Serves 4

Ingredients

- 1 tbsp sunflower oil
- 1 onion , chopped
- 1-2 tbsp chipotle paste (depending on how hot you like it)
- 2 x 400g cans black beans , drained and rinsed
- 400g can mixed bean , drained and rinsed
- 2 x 400g cans chopped tomatoes with garlic & herbs
- 1 heaped tbsp brown sugar
- 4 eggs
- small handful coriander leaves
- soured cream , to serve
- warm flour tortillas , to serve

Method

STEP 1

Heat the oil in a deep frying pan and cook the onion for about 5 mins until soft. Add the chipotle paste, beans, tomatoes and sugar, and simmer for about 15-20 mins until thickened. Season to taste.

STEP 2

Make 4 holes and crack an egg into each one. Cover and simmer over a low heat for 8-10 mins until the eggs are cooked to your liking. Sprinkle with coriander leaves and serve with a bowl of soured cream and some warm flour tortillas.

Spinach & chickpea curry

Prep:5 mins **Cook:**15 mins

Serves 4

Ingredients

- 2 tbsp mild curry paste
- 1 onion, chopped
- 400g can cherry tomatoes
- 2 x 400g cans chickpeas, drained and rinsed
- 250g bag baby leaf spinach
- squeeze lemon juice
- basmati rice, to serve

Method

STEP 1

Heat the curry paste in a large non-stick frying pan. Once it starts to split, add the onion and cook for 2 mins to soften. Tip in the tomatoes and bubble for 5 mins or until the sauce has reduced.

STEP 2

Add the chickpeas and some seasoning, then cook for 1 min more. Take off the heat, then tip in the spinach and allow the heat of the pan to wilt the leaves. Season, add the lemon juice, and serve with basmati rice.

Piri-piri chicken with smashed sweet potatoes & broccoli

Prep: 20 mins **Cook:** 55 mins

Ingredients

- 3 large sweet potatoes (about 900g), peeled and cut into large chunks
- oil , for drizzling
- 6-8 chicken thighs, skin left on
- 2 red onions , cut into wedges
- 25g sachet piri-piri spice mix (or a mild version, if you like)
- 300g long-stem broccoli

Method

STEP 1

Heat the oven to 180C/160C fan/gas 4. Toss the sweet potatoes with a generous drizzle of oil and some seasoning, and tip into a very large roasting tin. Push the potatoes to one end of the tin, then, in the other end, toss the chicken with the onions, spice mix, a drizzle of oil and some seasoning. Roast for 40 mins, stirring everything halfway through. Add the broccoli to the tin, drizzle with a little oil and season, then roast for 10-15 mins more.

STEP 2

Remove the chicken, onions and broccoli from the tin. Roughly mash the potatoes using a fork, making sure you incorporate all the chicken juices and spices from the pan. Spread the mash over the base of the tin, then top with the broccoli, chicken and onions and serve from the tin in the middle of the table.

Printed in Great Britain
by Amazon